MAYA
MONUMENTS

MAYA MONUMENTS

NIGEL HUGHES

ANTIQUE COLLECTORS' CLUB

The right of Nigel Hughes to be identified as author of this work has been
asserted by him in accordance with the Copyright, Designs and Patents Act 1988

British Library Cataloguing-in-Publication Data
A catalogue record for this book is available from the British Library

Frontispiece: El Tabasqueño. Principal Temple
Endpapers: Map of the Maya region

Every effort has been made to acknowledge the translator of the poem on page 145
but, to date, all attempts at identification have proved unsuccessful.

Printed in England by the Antique Collectors' Club Ltd., Woodbridge, Suffolk
on Consort Royal Satin paper supplied by the Donside Paper Company,
Aberdeen, Scotland

CONTENTS

The Colour Plates

The minor illustrations are taken from the author's site sketch books.

Xlabpak
Principal Temple

PREFACE

Returning by sea from New Zealand at the age of thirty, Nigel Hughes left his ship at Panama and took a turn through Mesoamerica which first brought the mighty ruins of Maya civilisation to his enraptured notice. Subsequently he made three further journeys into Maya territory, the two most productive being in 1982 and 1984, each of two months' duration, which furnished his portfolio with the drawings for the forty large watercolours which illustrate this book, and furnished his mind with the scholarship which gracefully informs the text. Some of the sites were accessible with ease, others could only be reached on foot, or by a dusty pillion-ride on the mayor's motorbike. Nigel Hughes did whatever was required in order to satisfy his curiosity and complete his drawings.

Hughes touches his cap in the direction of Frederick Catherwood, whose engraved pictures of some of the same subjects illustrated a book of travels made in the 1830s. But Catherwood reflects in his plates the Romantic taste of Europe in his day, which lends his rain forest the look of an exotic *pleasaunce* engulfing ruined summer-houses. Nigel Hughes represents what he sees with his clear modern eye. Where Catherwood gives nature a frisson of menace, and Maya sculpture a dreadful ferocity, Hughes's paintings are not possessed by such demons. He even manages to wring what looks suspiciously like a smile from one pair of stony lips.

Comments on the plates discuss most aspects of Maya civilisation. If, for instance, you ever wondered what games were played in their ball-courts, you will find here a concise exposition of all that is known in the matter. Behind an elegant pen, his learning is formidable. The book revives a tradition of scholarly travellers, who have the ability to enter imaginatively into the life of an ancient era, and to regret poignantly its mysterious disappearance into ruin. 'The course of history is muffled' (Hughes writes of the vanished Maya empire) 'like the legendary bells of sunken churches, whose tolling comes uncertainly through the swaying tides.'

Philip Glazebrook

Nakum – Structure A

ACKNOWLEDGEMENTS

My greatest inspiration for this work was Frederick Catherwood, who preceded me by 150 years at the Royal Academy Schools and who recorded ten ancient Maya sites (almost all that were then known to European travellers) during his journey with John Stephens in 1839. His originals were unfortunately destroyed by fire, but they survive in the form of highly accomplished coloured lithographs, as well as in the plates illustrating Stephens's book, *Incidents of Travel in Central America, Chiapas and Yucatan*.

People too numerous to name, looking after the ruins and defending them from theft and damage, often remote from government support, and others living near the sites, were not only very kind and hospitable but also funds of knowledge. The one I came to know best was Carlos Rodas, guardian of Yaxhá and Topoxte in Guatemala, and a most helpful and educative companion. I was given every possible assistance by the archaeological and history departments and museum staffs of Mexico, Guatemala, Honduras and Belize, and by field archaeologists and others whom I found working at several of the sites. William Folan of the University of Campeche and Francis Polo in Guatemala helped with access to some remote places.

John and Sarah Wiseman in Mexico City were perennially encouraging; in their house I collected myself before and after my journeys in the Maya area. Krister and Jel Göranson were similarly genial in Guatemala City, providing an affectionate base for travels in the Petén, an area not renowned for composure in the 1980s. In Belize the British armed forces provided generous hospitality, and half a dozen members supported my work by commissioning paintings. George and Janet Cobb were knowledgeable hosts in the Yucatan, while my friend of thirty years, Leopoldo Rebollar y Pliego, gave a most valuable historical perspective.

Greatly appreciated in 1988 was the invitation of the Museo Nacional de Antropología in Mexico, under the directorship of Eduardo Matos Moctezuma, to send the forty-one watercolours there for exhibition, with the very kind sponsorship of KLM-Royal Dutch Airlines and unfailing support from the British Council and Embassy. This exhibition had been preceded by one put on in 1987 by Intercultura of Fort Worth, at the National Arts Club in New York, generously helped on that occasion by Aer Lingus.

Dr Norman Hammond kindly looked through my writings at an early stage, but mine is the responsibility for any disputable material.

The late David Hicks generated the last stage of getting this book produced, introducing me with characteristic enthusiasm to Diana Steel of Antique Collectors' Club. Working with the people of that perfectionist firm has been a most congenial experience.

INTRODUCTION

In the archæology of America revisions are quite as common as new discoveries, and sometimes quite as sensational. Since my first excited sight of Copán, the suggested dates for man's arrival in the New World, from Siberia to Alaska, have been moved backwards by more than 16,000 years. Many aspects of Maya civilization can expect altered interpretations, and we shall sometimes be offered a choice of possibilities to consider, as science becomes more accessible and perhaps a little less didactic.

The remote ancestors of all the indigenous peoples of America walked across the isthmus which joined Asia to America in glacial times, the earliest appearing to have entered the new continent before 25,000 BC. Spreading through the land in groups, the migrants lived for millennia by hunting, fishing and gathering. Only when they settled in a particular territory did they gradually turn to a primitive (and egalitarian) agriculture. In spite of subsequent incursions from other areas, and of migrations through their realm, it appears that the first people to settle in the Maya lands were the progenitors of the Maya whose pre-Columbian civilization flourished so remarkably in the period illustrated by this book, and whose descendants still inhabit the region, numbering well over two million today. The stages in their development can be traced from astonishingly early times, and the dating of those stages is corroborated by discoveries in other parts of the Americas.

This prosaic account of the Mayas' origins negates a variety of extravagant earlier theories. In the eighteenth and nineteenth centuries it was suggested that the Maya arrived from overseas shortly before their great florescence, from places as diverse as the sunk Atlantis, India, Egypt and Israel (the Lost Tribe, who else?). Certainly there were influences from neighbouring cultures in Mesoamerica (a name coined and needed by archæologists to describe the area between northern Mexico and Costa Rica), but the main credit for their achievement belongs to the Maya themselves: for thousands of years they occupied the same lands, where they generated sufficient resources for intellectual and material advance on a grand scale.

The area covered by Maya culture (see map) includes the whole of modern Guatemala and Belize, the western parts of Honduras and El Salvador, and most of the five eastern states of Mexico. The terrain of this extensive region varies from a predominantly highland southern part to the level plains and occasional low hills of the Yucatán peninsula in the north. On the Pacific side of the continental divide there is a narrow coastal plain, the main route of southward migration in prehistoric times. From the plain, foot-hills rise rapidly to the mountains, many of which are violently volcanic. The highlands extend hundreds of miles northwards, with deep and well-separated valleys, until they fall away to a huge area of rain forest and savannah, drained by the Grijalva, Usumacinta and Candelaria river systems to the Gulf of Mexico, and by the rivers of Belize to the Caribbean Sea. Towards the northern part of the Yucatán peninsula, the land becomes drier and the natural vegetation turns to low forest and drought-resistant bush, characterized by thorniness and an abundance of cacti. Westwards along the Gulf of Mexico, the rich alluvial plains of Tabasco used to carry the rain forest and savannah to the coast but these have been largely cleared in historic times.

The climate is what you would expect from the terrain and the vegetation. In simplest terms, the highlands have a high rainfall, the rain forest rather less and the dry plains of Yucatán relatively little. Water for human use is less easily come by as one goes further north, until in the Yucatán it is practically never found at the surface, accumulating instead in subterranean caverns and obtainable only from sink-holes and wells. The rainy season is more pronounced in the north, and lasts roughly from May to October.

After ages of slow advance, the pace of Maya development seems to have quickened in the tenth millennium BC. The main periods of the ensuing culture have convenient labels: Archaic, Preclassic, Classic and Postclassic.

The Archaic runs from 9000 to 2000 BC, its onset marked by the appearance of various flaked stone tools. Agriculture and the selective breeding of useful plants began somewhere in the middle of that immense stretch of time, and the working of stone into useful shapes by abrasion started in the last millennium of the period, together with the making of pottery.

The Preclassic covers the period between 2000 BC and AD 250, and in it there were enormous advances. Because it lasts so well, broken or whole, some of the best evidence for the Mayas' growing achievement comes from their pottery, which everywhere began to acquire distinction and technical excellence, and from carved jades, their most precious artefacts. Jade (here in fact jadeite) is a beautifully coloured stone, mainly green, and much harder than a modern steel file, therefore immensely durable. It could only be fashioned in those Neolithic days by attrition with its own fragments: the working of it into complicated and lovely shapes by this laborious method always seems a wonderful accomplishment. Also in this period occurred a spectacular increase through breeding in the size of various food plants (the most important being maize), making possible large human settlements with a strong agricultural base.

In the early Preclassic the most ancient ceremonial buildings, erected for that particular purpose only, were built in stone and plaster on platforms of various shapes – the forerunners and often the foundations of the vast Classic period monuments. During the Preclassic the focus of Maya culture began to move from the highlands to the lowlands, where the rain forest centres were to

XCALUMKÍN
Classic Maya corbel vault

achieve their far-famed magnificence.

The Classic begins at AD 250 and ends, generally speaking, at AD 900. The dates were originally proposed with the idea that the period should contain the first to the last dated monuments in the rain forest sites. The original start was AD 300, the then earliest date to be found on a stela (stelæ are upright monoliths, usually sculpted), but this was revised in view of fresh discoveries. Even earlier dated inscriptions have now come to light, but further backward extension of the Classic (only a label, after all) would be confusing and serve little purpose. The beginning of the period coincides more or less with the invention of the corbelled stone vault and the appearance of multicoloured pottery. The end of the period is marked by the cessation of stelæ, (or, rather, their interruption, for more were raised at the northern sites in the Postclassic). Since the end of the Classic is a political fact, and occurred in a different year at each political centre, it is put at different times, according to location.

At any rate, the great ceremonial centres in the rain forest were abandoned one by one, for reasons far from clear even after a century and more of research and speculation. It is now thought that the governing classes may have taken themselves northward to the Gulf coast and into the Yucatán peninsula, where belongs the focus of the early Postclassic period. The civic life of several minor places in the rain forest did continue in a subdued form, but the close of the tenth century marks the end of an era for the Maya everywhere.

The monuments and artefacts of Postclassic Yucatán evince a decline from Classic purity, stylistically and technically. In the twelfth century the modes of art and religion were greatly changed, many would say debased, by peoples from the distant north-west, including the Toltecs. These were a belligerent people who invaded Chichén Itzá from the northern part of the Valley of Mexico, where their harsh original capital of Tula still exposes its huge and hideous sculptures to the sky. The Toltecs grafted their manners and customs on to the religion and æsthetics of the northern Maya; and the part of Chichén built under their dominance after AD 1100 seems to foreshadow the México-Tenochtitlán of the later Aztecs. The architecture took on a tougher line, while sculpture and painting were used to formalize the cruel religious practices then prevalent, notably human sacrifice on a grand scale. Meanwhile, away from this gaunt metropolis, building technique degenerated into shoddy layout and ramshackle execution. Towards AD 1250, Chichén Itzá was supplanted by Mayapán, a new city based on political confederation. In spite of the decay of artistry, cultural, political and economic activity continued, with a strong trade by land and sea to points far and wide in Mesoamerica and beyond. This commerce was largely conducted by the Putún Maya, whose main bases were coastal and who contrived to prosper through all the upheavals of the Postclassic. In 1502 Columbus's ship met one of their

HOCHOB – Temple 2

sea-going canoes in the Caribbean: it was an impressively well-found craft, laden with beautiful goods.

When the Spaniards finally arrived and set about destroying the old order, they did not find the Maya at all easy to subject: Tayasal, the last Maya stronghold in the Petén, was not finally overthrown until 1697, and Maya independence has asserted itself on several occasions since then.

Outside influences on the Maya have been mentioned, and these can be detected in buildings and artefacts from the Preclassic onwards. Building and sculptural styles indicate strong links with the Olmecs of Tabasco and Vera Cruz, and even a descent from them for some characteristic techniques and artistic idioms. Also from the Olmecs came the beginnings of the Maya system of numeration. There is a linguistic connection between the Maya and the Totonacs, whose principal extant monument is El Tajín in Vera Cruz. Trade goods discovered by archæologists show that there was contact with the contemporary Mixtec and Monte Albán cultures, and since traders throughout the area are known to have been protected by a universal convention, it seems likely that ideas were exchanged as well as goods. Teotihuacan in one direction and Costa Rica, possibly Panama, in the other, appear to have been the limits for Maya merchants, but it is unreasonable to rule out the possibility of contact with the civilizations of South America, especially in the Postclassic, when the Putún Maya were such competent mariners.

The large city of Teotihuacan in central Mexico was one of the most pervasive outside forces in Maya history, clear innovations from there being visible in the Classic art and architecture of several major Maya centres, particularly Tikal and Seibal. These things are easy to see, but it is not possible to tell how great was the political influence without a full translation of the inscriptions of that time. In the Postclassic the principal newcomers to the area were the Toltecs and allied tribes, just mentioned, who made such major changes to Maya culture, civic life and religion.

One might expect the Classic Maya to have influenced other peoples in other regions, but there is surprisingly little stylistic or other evidence that they did so. Cacaxtla near Puebla and Xochicalco near Cuernavaca exhibit purely Maya elements well outside the main Maya area, but both are completely isolated. There is much conjecture about a few similarities between certain monuments in Perú and some of the Maya ones, but these are hints rather than the arrival of a wholesale cultural force. While the Maya traded their artefacts far and wide, their special skills and techniques, the elegance of their art and their formidable intellectual achievements do not seem to have been widely exported. It may be that while their commonwealth attracted strangers, they had little inclination to colonize outside their own large realm.

On the basis that all civilizations have a rise, a flowering and a decline, the

LABNÁ
Arch from the south-east

Maya appear to have reached the high point of their assurance and artistic success in the Classic period. It is from those centuries that the most beautiful and numinous of their works derive, and to which our attention is most strongly drawn today. Even the largest and most politically important sites, like Tikal and Copán, produce copious evidence of humanity and individualism from that time, while the colossal dynastic sculptures seem intended to dignify their originals as well as to impress beholders. Different centres had lively individual styles, and artists were clearly striving to excel themselves and each other. We now know that much of the monumental art was dynastic propaganda and an instrument of political control, but every item of ornament is nonetheless imbued with meaning and vigour. The architecture is stately and confident, untainted by the decadent and unambitious spirit of later centuries, while sculpture, painting and pottery are seen at their noblest. We know from these art forms and from the early Spanish chronicles that music, dance and costume were highly developed and also considered important.

The achievements of the Maya are all the more remarkable in the light of their technical limitations. Chief among the latter were the absence of all metals, (except gold and copper, both mechanically useless, and which only appeared in the area in the tenth century AD), ignorance of the wheel (other than in toys, curiously) and a lack of draught animals. All the stone for building and sculpture had to be worked with other stone, chiefly obsidian (volcanic glass) and flint-like chert. All the moving and lifting of material had to be done in the most primitive manner. One assumes that at least the roller, the lever and the wedge were in use, especially when considering huge pieces of stone like Stela E at Quiriguá, which weighs about 64 tons and was quarried at some distance from the site.

The true curved arch was unknown to the Maya (just as it was unknown to the ancient Greeks). Doorways were spanned by simple wooden or stone lintels, and interior spaces were vaulted by corbelling, this feature giving much of its character to their architecture. The free-standing ceremonial arches referred to later were built in the same way.

The Maya do not appear to have fully grasped the best way of bonding masonry, and this must have been a great impediment to them in their work. Many of their walls have fallen apart at continuous vertical joints, and the majority of sites are full of courses of stonework laid without regard to the breaks in the courses below.

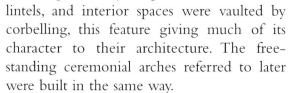

Fer-de-lance
(Bothrops mummifer)

UXMAL
House of the Tortoises

YAXCHILÁN
Structure 33

There are two lines of descent from the lowly Archaic-period house, raised on its earth platform to keep the floor dry. The first line runs virtually unaltered through all the ages into the twentieth century. The shapes of houses in the earliest Archaic can be seen from old post-holes in the remains of their platforms: precisely similar houses are being built and inhabited throughout the rural parts of the Maya area today. Interestingly, humble thatched dwellings of the same pattern are represented on the façades of several Classic ceremonial buildings, notably at Chicanná, Uxmal and Labná.

The other line of development leads from the original simple house, with a place set apart in it for religious observances, to the grand temples of the Classic period on their towering pyramids. Buildings are found to have been reserved for devotion in the Preclassic, and, as one might expect, they were designed to stand pre-eminent in their surroundings. Very early on came the practice of founding a larger temple on a smaller one, completely burying the latter. It is now known at what stage these reconstructions started to celebrate calendric cycles, from the documentary evidence of the inscribed stelæ and other stone monuments of the Classic period, and from related burials. The dates on the inscribed stones are normally separated by periods of ten or twenty years, the latter being a major unit in the Maya reckoning of time. The temples were generally rebuilt in rotation so that each one would last several cycles until its turn for refurbishment came round again. Excavations have revealed temple pyramids whose outer surfaces encase seven or eight others within. As the temples and pyramids grew ever larger, the task of covering them with new ones must have been increasingly daunting, although one imagines that it would have been thought most unfitting to have started a new smaller building with larger and older ones all around. The whole operation was an act of worship, with only the best being good enough for the gods, but it may be that the labourers did not always share the enthusiasm of those in charge. Combined with other causes, popular dismay at the programme of public works is likely to have had something to do with the abandonment of the great rain forest centres.

As the Classic advanced, so did the sophistication of the ornament: the stairways and flights of steps became ever more stately and impressive, the sculpture in stucco and stone stood out in deeper relief, with an increasing boldness and complexity of design. Sufficient assurance was acquired in vaulting to enable the making of wide interior chambers. This was the only technique available for making masonry ceilings, apart from simply covering the space with a stone lid, as in a tomb.

The vault (see illustration of Xcalumkín on page 17) dictated the form of the entire building. Where the slope of the ceiling began, an inwards overhang was developed, each ascending course of stones being nearer to the centreline of the chamber. When the sides had been brought sufficiently close to each other,

LABNÁ
Corner of Palace

Great Curassows
(Crax rubra) female
above, male below

the gap was closed with a row of capstones. However, until that stage was reached, the inward-leaning masonry had to be counterbalanced by increasingly massive stonework towards the outside of the building. This is the reason for the ponderous higher levels of Maya buildings. A virtue was made of necessity, however, for they developed a convention of emphasizing and adorning the exteriors of these upper parts with architraves and cornices enclosing deep friezes, in tune with the underlying planes and masses. On the friezes exuberant serpentine forms and masks bristling with fangs alternate with restrained geometric patterns, and sometimes these rectilinear patterns themselves are mixed with others to set up an austere harmony. Whether by instinct or by calculation, the Classic Maya evolved a very pleasing canon of proportion. It strikes the same true note as do the most successful buildings of ancient Greece and Egypt, and it is interesting to search the Maya façades for Golden Sections, dynamic rectangles and other manifestations of planned harmony. This undeniable beauty of form led to some of the exotic proposals of origin made for the Maya and mentioned above; but it seems more generous to suggest that harmony is universal and that it has always been within the reach of everybody, than that it must emanate from any single cultural source.

Returning to the vaulted buildings, once the capstones were laid and sealed with mortar, there was a large surplus of structural strength, and this must have led to the invention of the roof-combs which are such a proud feature of Classic Maya architecture. These lofty crests could exceed the height of the sanctuaries they surmounted, and being relatively weak from front to back, they were often pierced with holes to let the wind through. In some localities they were solid single walls, in others they were double, the two component leaves being tied across the void at intervals with long stones. They were often provided with tenons as a foundation for relief work in stucco, sometimes for almost free-standing figures. Most of the sculptures have collapsed long since, leaving the tenons projecting.

While the temples on their pyramids are the most spectacular and awe-inspiring of the monuments, all the great ceremonial centres have ranges of other large-scale buildings. Of these, the largest and most stately have been variously termed 'palaces' and 'monasteries', from a European assumption that they were built for habitation by royal groups or religious communities. They contain rows of vaulted chambers, lit from outside only by their doorways. Sometimes they are set out round courtyards, sometimes they present a single straight façade to the landscape. At one or two sites, notably at Sayil and Etzná, terraces of rooms are incorporated into the pyramids, where they give a many-storeyed effect, while at Tikal there are buildings which actually do have two and three storeys. At the same place are seen rows of rooms arranged three or four deep.

In the north there survive two isolated arches, triumphal in note, and it seems likely that these are survivors of a greater number, since their form will have made them an easier prey to the forces of tropical nature than the more massive mound-based structures. Perhaps rare for the same reason are towers, of which there are very few: the most famous are an elegant and much-restored rectangular one at Palenque, and the cylindrical Caracol at Chichén Itzá.

At almost every site there are ball courts, whose use is illustrated in sculpture and pottery. The size of the court and its design varies from place to place, round a basic arrangement of two parallel walls.

One of the decorative delights of architecture is the interplay of sunlight and shadow, and none seem to have enjoyed it more than the Maya. The bold relief of their ornament, the alternation of level and inclined planes in the terracing, the sun-barred stairways, the emphatic masks and effigies, all are enhanced by strong light and deep shadows, which often produce telling subsidiary patterns. However, what is to be seen today is only a part of the original magnificence: all the masonry was once covered with white and coloured plaster. Most of the plaster has now disintegrated, but the surviving pieces are sufficient to show how expert were the Maya in this medium.

Colours had a religious significance, and apart from each cardinal direction having an associated colour, red was also the colour of mourning, black had to do with fasting, blue with rain and the rain gods, green with the centre of the universe, and so on, doubtless with a complexity of alternative connections. Certain temples are found to have been completely reddened at some stage, and it may be that they were simply washed over with an earth pigment for the occasion of a dedicatory burial. Traces of polychrome survive on some of the exterior friezes and roof-combs, but they are only fragments of an unimaginably splendid whole.

The seasonally waterlogged floor of the rain forest caused the Maya to make causeways in the ceremonial precincts, and occasionally outside them. Indeed, now that research is less concentrated on the spectacular centres of civilization, more of such roads are being found. The longest so far discovered runs straight westwards for sixty-two miles from the large site of Cobá in the north-east of the Yucatán peninsula. The roads at Cobá give a hint of strong political and economic control, exercised

over a wide area by a central metropolis; and perhaps they also served to keep outlying populations aware of the sacred alignments used in the ceremonial centres. However, there being neither wheeled traffic nor pack animals to require paved surfaces – the Cobá roads are unusual – the full extent and location of the Maya traffic-routes may never now emerge from the forest and bush which have swallowed them.

Only quite recently have the ancient Maya been recognized as expert farmers. It used to be taken for granted that all the Preclassic and Classic Maya followed the same system of agriculture as that practised today on family units of land in that part of the world, and known as *milpa* or cut-and-burn. This system has various unsoundnesses, and archæologists were exercised for many years as to how the large non-agricultural populations of the big centres were provided for. The question of subsistence is a subject on its own but suffice it to say that the Maya are now known to have farmed intensively and efficiently, and that their highly developed agriculture was the foundation of their civic achievement. On the other hand, there is sad proof that serious organizational flaws undermined the vast superstructure of their statecraft. Analysis of human bones shows that towards the close of the Classic the main population were relatively less well-nourished than either their forefathers or their own rulers. Moreover, for all their agricultural engineering, there may have been a fatal misunderstanding of the geography of their realm. A suggestion has been made, far-fetched perhaps, but not impossible, that the present rain-forest swamps were originally lakes with easily managed intensive farms round the shores and plentiful fish in the water, and that this system was suddenly ruined by a disastrous lowering of water levels, caused by a geological freak at the close of the ninth century AD.

The debate on the reasons for the upheaval at the end of the Classic period has been long, interesting and at times quite heated. Viewed from the precarious heights of a later civilization, the question has a certain immediacy, and it must be good for us to consider every possible cause for the dissolution of such grandeur. There is no archæological proof of epidemic disease, which in any case would have emptied the rain forest centres in a shorter period than the century or so which has to be accounted for. A more likely prime reason is popular dissatisfaction with the demands of the rulers. Those ever-increasing temples may have much to answer for, in the same way that the excessive demands by the Aztec priesthood from the people of sixteenth century Mexico made victory much easier for Cortés and his Spaniards. Admittedly, the burden in México-Tenochtitlán was more dramatic, consisting of enormous human sacrifices, but the situations are comparable in that both were engendered by theocracies. Although human sacrifice was practised by the Classic Maya, it is not thought to have been on a large scale: to judge by the arrangement of their

KOHUNLICH – Plaster masks

remains, it was a matter in which the victim's individuality retained its value, unlike the killing of thousands which Bernal Díaz and others describe as having taken place during the reign of Moctezuma.

Nonetheless, the monuments of the Maya must have required quite as much work as the temples of the Aztecs (it has been estimated that the large El Tigre pyramid at El Mirador in Guatemala required five million man-days of labour to construct), and the system of government at the end of the Classic must have been enormously more oppressive and less a matter of general consent than in earlier centuries.

It is unlikely that the Classic Maya were ever eclipsed over their whole area by war, either among themselves or from outside. In general (until the nineteenth century, one could say), when one American culture has impinged on another, there has been an assimilation of the dominated people and their accomplishments (as with the Toltec and the Maya round Chichén Itzá) rather than a complete extinction of conquered by conqueror. War between independent and aggressive-minded states was certainly much practised, as can be seen from the paintings at Bonampak, from hieroglyphic texts commemorating victories and from defensive works at sites like Becán, Tulum and Chichén, but it appears to have been on the level of raids by select military groups rather than combative movements of whole populations. The wars seem to have been to do with succession to kingships or conducted with a view to expansion when productive land was wanted by the aggressor.

As has been said, the ability of the Maya to write down their thoughts and activities enabled them to leave behind a huge body of records. The hieroglyphs made up a syllabary rather than an alphabet, and numbers (see page 34) had an alternative hieroglyphic representation. The glyphs had objective meanings as well as representing sounds, and there was a great deal of punning in the texts between the two sides of this duality. Hieroglyphic texts were inscribed on stone and plaster in buildings and on stelæ and altars, painted on tomb walls and pottery and written in folding books made of vegetable fibre. There were many hundreds of these books extant at the time of the Spanish conquest of the Yucatán, but the anti-heathen zeal of the Christian church led to the burning of practically all these writings in a series of inquisitorial bonfires. There are only four left, of which all but one are from the Postclassic period. The three later ones consist entirely of sacred almanacs, and the earliest is in such a bad state of preservation that no one knows how to restore it to legibility. It is some consolation that the texts on the monuments are becoming clearer as the decades pass. At one time it was thought that they consisted entirely of astronomical observations, a view encouraged by the very precise dates which were the first elements to be deciphered. Nowadays we see that the inscriptions are mainly records of dynastic history, although there is always a danger of confusing prophesy with event. Their original purpose was to reinforce the divine right of the rulers through descent from the gods, and legitimacy through descent from previous royal personages. Historians have been able to pick up long lines of succession from one ruler to another and records of marriages between members of great families, often from widely separated sites (the last ruler of Copán, for example, married a wife from Palenque), reading from several different monuments at each place. The inscriptions on the pottery and the activities pictured are often from a sacred literature and mythology, and they are probably the nearest we shall get to the undoubted riches contained in those tragically lost books.

The texts and the dates have shown that the Maya were enthusiastic and able astronomers. Undoubtedly their interest was in astrology, rather than a pure and disinterested study, but, liking to do things well, they succeeded in making many accurate and fascinating computations, of solar, lunar and planetary cycles, of eclipses and conjunctions and of the declination of the earth towards various heavenly bodies, although they must have seen things the other way round, with themselves at the centre of the cosmic scheme. Much of their architecture was affected by these observations, and their skill in this field is amply proved, both in the texts and in the alignment of buildings. It used to be supposed that the Maya were unable to set out a right angle in the plans of their temples and that anything between 80° and 100° was good enough; but it is far more likely, considering their deification of the cardinal points, that these skilled mathematicians regarded an accurate 90° as some sort of solecism and deliberately avoided it. Certainly the levels and verticals in the buildings do not support any theory of incompetence.

The pre-Christian religions of Mesoamerica had many features in common. They all observed certain calendars, the most prominent being based on the lunar month, the solar year and a 260 day cycle, observed since the deepest antiquity and kept up to this day in certain highland areas. Since the solar year lasts a fraction of a day over 365, it requires an intercalation, which the pre-Hispanic Americans provided skilfully enough, adding days as necessary throughout their history. The concept of the universe as a layered structure was held by all the peoples of the region, heaven and the underworld being ascribed several tiers above and below the earth. Common to many, also, was a belief that the world has been created and destroyed a number of times. However, each culture had its own labels for the gods, and even if the various deities were perhaps universally identifiable, their cults differed widely.

The Maya pantheon has been skilfully investigated and described elsewhere, largely by Sir Eric Thompson. It was an extremely complex affair, for almost every human activity had a divine patron or mentor, from rain-gods for agriculture to gods for childbirth and death. Rather like the dryads and nereids

stood for 3

stood for 10

stood for 17

stood for 20

stood for 60

(400s)

(20s)

(units)

stood for 466

of the Greeks and the djinni of the Arab world, there were lesser immortals, whose benevolence appears at times to have been somewhat suspect. It is thought that towards the close of the Classic, the religious thought of the Maya turned to the concept of one particular god being supreme and incorporeal, and on the whole benevolent. Nevertheless, the essence of all worship was an everlasting programme of keeping on the right side of many supernatural forces, with scope for expressing gratitude for past blessings as well as praying and sacrificing for the future. As long as their civilization lasted, the hieratic system gave the priests the role of interpreting the auguries and directing the worship of the ignorant. One assumes that the priests were also the astronomers and that their observations formed the basis for their divinations and for the complicated and far-reaching almanacs which are found as monumental inscriptions and in the very few surviving sacred books.

There has been much ethnographic research into the religious observances of the modern Maya, whose Christianity is often tinged with pre-Christian traditions. It cannot be altogether wrong to trace back to their ancient Maya ancestors some of the customs and attitudes seen today, particularly as so many can be found in the colonial records of the Spaniards. Seeing beyond all kinds of minor sacrifices, many of them extremely bizarre, there emerges a sense of dignified respect for the natural world, for each other and for themselves, on the part of the people described. This accords so ill with the heartless practices reported of the metropolitan Toltecs and Aztecs, that one is forced to view the latter as short-lived aberrations, caused by panic in the face of an apparently enraged cosmos or by some dreadful poisoning of the collective unconscious. Certainly, the pre-Christian prayers and poems which survive from all over Mesoamerica reveal dignity, humanity and love.

The Maya must have developed their arithmetic far beyond the basic level in order to serve their astronomy rather than for the more mundane purposes of architecture and trade. They took their system of numeration from the Olmec, but themselves evolved the enormous scope which it came to have in the Classic period. The system was based on the number twenty (vigesimal, therefore), with three symbols: a dot, a bar and a shell-shaped cipher. The dot was for units, used up to four at a time. The bar represented five, and was used up to three at a time. The shell was for completion, i.e. attainment of twenty or a multiple of twenty. It is now thought that the completion sign was also used as a zero in calculations. Examples of the symbols are shown on this page in the margin.

Naturally, a place shift of the completion sign produces a proportionately greater increase than in a decimal system. Thus, Maya numbers go 20, 400, 8000 rather than 10, 100, 1000.

The Maya were apparently able to add, subtract, multiply and divide, although they never understood fractions. Enormous figures running into many millions are

CHICHÉN ITZÁ
'El Caracol'

occasionally found in the texts. The days and years were parcelled up in lesser and greater periods, for the system of dating called the Long Count.

Although the whole area occupied by the Classic Maya used to be referred to as the Old Empire, it is evident that the region was divided into separate states, sometimes in alliance with each other, sometimes at odds. There were conquests and dynastic unions. Each major centre influenced surrounding centres in a feudal system of diminishing lordships, every unit down to the family having someone in charge who was answerable to a higher authority. Apart from slavery, which clearly existed, the system of raising labour for building operations is far from clear, but the easiest to conjecture is one of feudal service, which could be paid either in goods or labour.

Judging by population studies at major centres like Tikal, the Classic Maya were a great deal more numerous than their present rural descendants. Much of what is now high forest was cleared in their time for agriculture, so that one can postulate a widespread and large country population round densely inhabited settlements, which might be called cities or at least towns. Centres such as Tikal and Seibal are supposed at their height to have had populations of at least 10,000 people. Since those days, the vegetation of the whole Maya area has changed appreciably, due largely to human exploitation, and the rainfall pattern has probably altered also. While the ancient Maya sites in that area must have been sustained by intensive agriculture and in some cases aquaculture, today's xerophytic bush in the north and the huge tracts of rain forest further south are not hospitable to many of the enterprises of modern man. In consequence, hundreds of square miles which were formerly populous are nowadays practically deserted.

Today all Maya sites are under the control of national governments, and many have been restored or at least partially cleared so that they can be visited and seen. But at all but the most popular and famous, such as Chichén Itzá and Uxmal, the feeling persists that they are closely invested by the forest, which is only biding its time before re-occupying the ruins and covering them as completely as if they had never been disturbed.

Scarlet Macaw *(Ara macao)*

COBÁ – Nohuch Mul

'That great antiquity America *lay buried for thousands of years; and a large part of the earth is still in the Urne unto us.'*

Sir Thomas Browne, *HYDRIOTAPHIA* (1658).

COPÁN
*Principal Ball
Court*

THE VALLEY SITE OF COPÁN

The character and scale of Copán are best appreciated by walking right through it and only later settling to detailed inspection. A lovely river winds round one side of the site and gives it much of its romantic ambience, which is further enhanced by gigantic trees growing around and on the principal pyramids. These gradually give way to the disorder of normal tropical woodland at the edges of the ceremonial area: the archæological zone is seen from outside as an island of forest in a wide highland valley, where mixed agriculture and grazing are practised by a population of careful farmers. Fields of maize, beans, squash and tobacco occupy the level lands near the river, while the steeper slopes are given over to tree-shaded coffee and pasturage. Higher still, the ridges are covered with thorny bush and pine forest. The nearby village is the remotest in the valley, with only a rough road going up beyond to a mountain pass and the frontier with Guatemala. This *fin-de-ligne* situation makes it a place of peace and quiet retreat.

In Preclassic and Classic times, Copán was pre-eminent in a large area of what is now the Republic of Honduras, and a great centre of civic and religious activity. Its buildings are many and various – temples on huge pyramidal mounds, ball courts, long terraces like grand-stands, various curious arrangements of steps. All these are disposed round spacious rectangular courts, set out in such a way that in passing from one to the next, the visitor is aware of distinct but subtle changes of character in the spaces around him.

The Great Plaza, as it is called, is peopled with magnificent stelæ, upright monoliths, most of them behind low stone altars. The stone of the buildings and statuary is a beautiful green trachyte, relatively easy to work when fresh, but hardening with exposure.

Stone walls belonging to originally thatched buildings of a more secular type are found in quadrangular groups outside the ceremonial centre. Beyond these are the remains of innumerable humble dwellings, built of transitory materials and detectable only by systematic excavation. A mile or two away from the centre, in several directions, are outlying stelæ, probably beside ancient approach roads.

The pyramids of Copán were provided with fine stairways, many of them thrown apart during many centuries of abandonment by the growth and collapse of trees. The carved component stones lie everywhere, prominent among them being the frowning and fleshless head of death. It is curious how these baleful skulls, which lurk in odd corners all over the site, having lost their place in the architecture, have also lost their power to horrify.

COPÁN – Stela N and Altar N

There is one enormous flight of sixty-three steps, whose risers made up a single enormous text of over 2,500 hieroglyphs. Sadly, as no one knew how to read it at the time of its original restoration, and as it was very ruined, it was assembled in a random order. If ever the writing comes to be fully deciphered, rearranging the stones correctly will be an intriguing exercise.[1]

Copán was the first Maya ruin to be visited by John Lloyd Stephens and Frederick Catherwood in 1839. Then and now, there could be no more inspiring place to begin a study of the ancient Maya, for the growth of this extinct city of theirs seems to have been arrested at the moment of its most perfect flowering.

1. *There is now a project to make this rearrangement. (Author)*

DYNASTIC MEMORIALS

The effigies on the Copán stelæ are in deeper relief than at any other Maya site, some of them being almost in the round. They are memorials of powerful hieratic dynasts, rulers whose assured and level regard still radiates authority after the lapse of over a millennium.

The figures are shown richly clad in a complicated regalia of jade, jaguar-skin and quetzal feathers. Cylinders and beads of jade, pierced by laborious drilling, were sewn together to make a kind of latticework kilt. Magnificent belts, collars, ear-flares and ornaments for knee and wrist were made of the same precious material. The quetzal, *Pharomachrus mocinno,* is now a rare bird restricted almost entirely to the Alta Verapaz area of highland Guatemala, but it was always hard to catch and highly prized. Its feathers were made into huge head-dresses, whose plumes flowed down the back and sides of the wearer in cascades of iridescent green. One wonders if any attempt was made to imitate the original colour of the feathers when the stelæ were painted for their first dedication. The few vestiges of stucco that remain are red, yellow and white. Red was the colour of mourning, and many monuments were overpainted or repainted in that colour to mark some dismal event.

The personages on the stelæ generally carry a ceremonial bar or sceptre, held horizontally across their chests. The bars terminate in grotesque heads and it appears that the originals were frequently made of flint, skilfully pressure-flaked to arrive at involved silhouettes.

Hieroglyphic inscriptions occur on the sides of some of the stelæ and on the backs of others, also on their pedestals. Many stelæ have two effigies back to back, Janus-like.

At Copán, and at many other sites, the human figures appear to have undergone a subtle change of proportion: they are curiously reminiscent of certain predatory animals, notably the jaguar. The Maya greatly admired this animal for its power and cunning. In addition to using its skin as an élitist uniform, it looks as though they decided to endow the subjects of their statuary with jaguar traits. These amount to a thickening of the limbs, a stately ponderosity of the head and a slight but telling adjustment in the proportions of legs and arms. The jaguar's back leg between stifle and hock is much longer in proportion to the whole leg than the same limb in animals more dependent on sustained speed, such as the ocelot or the puma, and this characteristic may

COPÁN – Stela D and Altar D

be seen in the effigies. The connection with the animal is further emphasized by frequent jaguar references in the hieroglyphs for the rulers' names, combinations such as 'Bird Jaguar' and 'Sky Jaguar'.

The texts on twenty-three of the stelæ and sixteen of the altars, as well as seven other dedicatory inscriptions, have been sufficiently deciphered to show that they commemorated events in the reigns of only five rulers. The custom before the accession of the first of these people had been to destroy all antecedent memorials, but the second of the five abolished the custom, with the result that there is a series of dated monuments spanning the years from AD 613 to 800. Surprisingly perhaps, it turns out that many of the altars were dedicated much later than their attendant stelæ.

In the Grand Plaza is a group of altars rather odder than the rest; a stone tortoise with huge claws and two heads of hideous malignity, a square stone carved as a corded package, and a round stone like a bun, with a turban round its equator and channels (drainage for the blood of sacrifices?) running spirally down from the top.

On the buildings the relief carving is complemented by true statuary, free-standing figures of great virtuosity. Although they used to be rather monotonously labelled 'Heads of the Young Maize God' the human busts appear to be portraits, strongly stylized but full of individuality and charm.

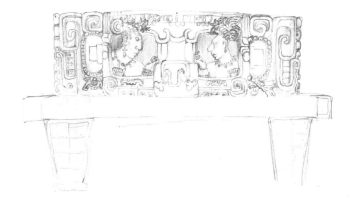

Carved stone bench at Copán

THE MAYA BALL GAME

Practically every Maya site has at least one ball court and many places have several. There is a basic pattern, but they vary in design from the huge enclosed rectangle at Chichén Itzá with its towering side walls and pavilions, to modest structures like the one at Yaxchilán, which for all the grandeur of its surroundings is almost as plain an example as possible: a simple arrangement of two long parallel mounds, faced with stone to give plane surfaces inclined towards the central axis. Common to all is this channel of masonry, up and down which the game was played. The ends of the court do not seem to have been as important in the scoring of the game as the markers, which were placed along the sides and centre line of the court, with the principal goal rings generally halfway between ends. Early records show the floor of the court divided into different coloured rectangles.

The most ancient courts were built and played in by the Olmecs, near the Gulf Coast of Mexico, and from there the custom spread throughout Mesoamerica. The essential starting point must have been the discovery that a splendidly resilient ball could be made from the smoke-coagulated sap of an indigenous tree, *Castilla elastica*.[1]

At its most intense the contest was not really a game at all, in the sense that modern football or hockey are games. For a comparison one has to think of solemn occupations such as the *corridas* of Spain or the bull-vaulting of Minoan Crete: all these might be better described as adversarial rituals than as sports. The relief carvings at Chichén and at other courts show a sacrifice of the captain of one of the teams, supposedly the winning one, his severed neck sending up plant shoots in token of his sacrificial death bringing life to his people. The religious aspect is emphasised by the fact that old ball courts were frequently buried under fresh ones, like the temple pyramids. The principal court at Copán is the third of three successive stages.

The nineteenth century French explorer Desiré Charnay sensibly referred to the game as tennis, presumably having in mind real tennis. He chose it as the nearest European equivalent, with its complicated scoring and sloping surfaces built into the court.

Just as the Maya had regional designs of court, so they must have had regional styles of play and scoring. The number of people in each of the two teams depended on the size of the court, and perhaps on the importance of the match: probably anything between three-a-side on a small court and dozens on a huge court like the one at Chichén Itzá. The ball was only supposed to be struck with knee, hip or elbow, which were protected by guards. It may be that

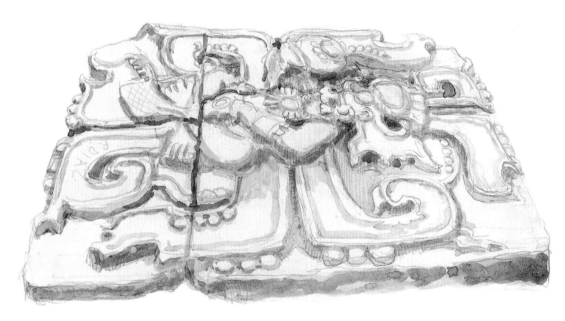

Copán: ball court centre line marker

players were only allowed to strike in strict turns and unassailed by opponents, which would have made aiming a little easier; but, considering the size of the holes in the goal-stones, it is no wonder that goals were rare and that the majority of the scoring points depended on lesser feats. The chronicles say that apart from instantly securing victory for his team, a player putting the ball through the central marker was customarily entitled to the clothes of the opposition and of all the spectators.

The costume worn for important games was stately. Apart from rich clothes and head-dresses, the joint guards were made of various ornamental materials, such as painted wood, carved and polished stone, or even jade. These trappings have survived in burials, particularly the U-shaped hip-guards. It used to be thought that these stone objects were purely ceremonial, since they weighed as much as forty pounds; but it now appears that they were worn for actual play. Blade-shaped stone objects called *hachas* (axes), and others of a curious palmate shape have also been found in tombs. All these were further pieces of games gear, worn at the waist in conjunction with the stone hip-guards.

In the Maya area the game has long been extinct. Bishop Landa describes nothing of the kind in his annals of the newly colonized Yucatán, so it can be assumed that it came to an end in those parts during Post-Classic times. However, there remains one small area in north-west Mexico where it does survive, among the Indians of coastal Sinaloa and Nayarit. They have no courts, but they play with a rubber ball in a long field, striking the ball only with hip or thigh. Their tradition has a history of at least three thousand years.

1. The plant from which modern rubber is obtained, Hevea brasiliensis, *comes, as its name suggests, from South America rather than from this region.*

Copán: ball court side markers

THE SITE OF QUIRIGUÁ

The ruins of Quiriguá lie among the banana farms of the lower Motagua valley. The archæological zone is an island of dense woodland, on level ground, with glades cleared round the principal monuments. In this small forest there thrives a rich wildlife, protected by the custodians of the site and by the neighbouring landowners.[1] The monuments are all the more attractive for being enlivened by the flight of toucans and parrots, and their singing and chattering pervade the daylight hours. In the dying light of dusk these sounds deepen and carry further, making a fitting music for the relics of a tropical kingdom.

The first thing to astonish the visitor is the enormous height of the stelæ. The main group contains three particularly tall ones, of which the largest is Stela E, 35 feet high and calculated to weigh over 60 tons. It is the biggest monolithic monument in the New World.[2]

The ceremonial precinct also contains a series of four zoomorphic monuments. These are gigantic and grotesque animal forms, whose features derive from saurian, avian, reptilian, feline and perhaps other originals. The piece in the illustration borrows most from the toad, albeit an extravagantly fabulous one. Like the stelæ, the zoomorphs are dynastic memorials: the human heads and figures incorporated in the sculptures are certainly portraits. The same ruler is probably represented on all four stones, although they are too eroded now for recognition. Secondary heads, seen emerging from the back ends of the creatures, are likely to be portraits of predecessors or consorts. While these monuments are fashioned in exceedingly complicated patterns, a large part of their strength as sculpture is due to the carving being superficial, in the sense that the stones have been left as far as possible in their original accidental shapes. They are dated from AD 780 to 795, one every five years. They occur after a series of stelæ, and the stelæ are briefly resumed after them, one for 800 and one for 805, the last at Quiriguá.

On all the monuments, the carved hieroglyphs are of superb quality, cut into a reddish sandstone of uneven grain. In its surface the sculptors have placed designs of surpassing inventiveness and assurance. Conventional hieroglyphics frequently give way to amazing compositions of mythical creatures, but confined to the same panelled format as the glyphs. Every conceivable freak of Maya dæmonology is involved in this florid substitute for the more usual mode of Maya writing. One can suggest an analogy with the richly embroidered initial letters of early European manuscripts, particularly those in the Celtic tradition. In view of this exuberance, it is rather surprising that the human heads and figures on the stelæ are so much more formalized than those at Copán, little more than thirty miles away across the mountains to the south, and a place which had close links with Quiriguá at the time when the monuments were raised.

1. Del Monte S. de R.L. de Guatemala.
2. The second tallest is at Nimli Punit in Belize, thought never to have been raised and to have been intentionally broken owing to a calendrical error in its inscribed date.

QUIRIGUÁ
Zoomorph G

MAYA DATES

The Maya had a strong instinct for order, which led them to pay keen attention to the passage of time and to look for markers in the heavens by which they could divide the flow of days and years. Consummate astronomers, they measured various planetary cycles, notably the solar year, the lunar year and the Venus year, whose mutual coincidences they observed and recorded in written almanacs, practically all now lost or destroyed. Their achievements in this field were more accurate than anywhere else in the world until the invention of the telescope. Proof of this is the fact that they understood the necessity for intercalation rather better than Europeans, who did not abolish the faulty Julian calendar until the eighteenth century (replacing it with the still not quite right Gregorian one).

Their major non-solar calendar comprised 260 days. The start of one of these periods coincides once every fifty-two years with the start of a solar year, and fifty-two years thus became the most important time cycle in Mesomerica. The observance of the turn of one of these great calendars by the Aztecs is amply recorded in the early Spanish chronicles, and the fatalistic acceptance of Cortés by the Mexicans was largely due to his arrival at that moment of omen.

The dating system used in Maya inscriptions is called the Long Count. It is made up of five elements (like days, months and years in modern dating), and as a rule these are arranged to read downwards. From the top, they give *baktun*s of 144,000 days (approximately 400 years) each, *katun*s of approximately twenty years, *tun*s (approximate years of 360 days), *uinal*s (twenty day months) and *kin*s, days. In the date inscriptions, each element occurs in a number up to nineteen, twenty being completion in the vigesimal system of Maya arithmetic, and causing an increase of one in the next element up. Although the dates are approximate if read directly as years, the count of days was absolutely accurate and ran from a starting point in the remote past, computed by a succession of modern scholars[1] to be the thirteenth of August, 3114 BC. This is long before the time of inscribed records and of the mathematical decision which established that distant beginning.

The earliest dated monument so far discovered in the lowlands is Stela 29 at Tikal, with a Long Count date of AD 292; and the earliest sculpted date found anywhere in the Maya area is AD 126, from Abaj Takalik on the Pacific side of the Guatemalan mountains. All the dates fall in the 8th, 9th and 10th *baktun*s, although there was high excitement at one stage when a stone was discovered with an apparent 7 in the *baktun* space, altering the date by four hundred years. As the *baktun* is the uppermost element in the inscription, it is normally the most subject to erosion. A 9 (••••) can easily be worn into a

7 ($\overset{\bullet\bullet}{\rule{1.2em}{1pt}}$)[2], which is almost certainly what happened in this case.

In addition to the bar and dot numerals, there were equivalent hieroglyphs, 1 to 20. Some dates consist of bar and dot figures on their own, some have the two systems side by side and some are expressed in hieroglyphics only.

The Maya concept of the calendar was of a series of divine beings carrying the periods of time as loads. Each bore his day, his month or whatever period was in his charge for its appointed course, before handing it over to his successor (again, the concept of completion as found in the Maya system of numeration). And so it went on forever, a heavenly relay system, in which the carriers returned to their responsibilities in reassuring and predictable order.

It is only fair to say that the most generally accepted correlation with the Christian calendar is open to a small degree of doubt. Presumably the matter would be finally settled if some fixed celestial event, such as the recurrent passage of a comet, were to be found dated in Maya records. For instance, Halley's comet, noted elsewhere in the world on many of its periodic visits during those centuries, must have been clearly visible in the Maya lands. It is tantalizing to think that it may well have been recorded in some of the almanacs which the early Spaniards so enthusiastically destroyed.

1. The correlation is known as the Goodman-Martínez-Thompson, so called after the three scholars who developed it, Joseph Goodman, Juan Martínez Hernández and J. Eric S. Thompson.
2. See Introduction, page 34.

LOOTING

Once discovered, the monuments are vulnerable from two very different agents of deterioration: the weather and the looter.

A piece of limestone newly unearthed and left in the open is liable to rapid erosion by the elements. Sadly, for the look of the thing, this means that a roof has to be provided, to mitigate the ill effects of alternating sun and rain, and of widely varying temperatures. Roofs can be dispensed with if enough trees can be left growing on the site to give shelter, but this is not always easy to manage in combination with large-scale works of excavation and restoration. Of course, there are roofs and roofs, and they do not need to be unsightly structures of steel scaffolding and corrugated iron. When the site guardians are left to their own devices, as at Nakum in Guatamela, the resulting thatches on slender poles give the rather charming feeling of shrines in the wilderness – a happy compromise. All the same, total preservation is impossible and the monuments are bound to suffer from exposure.

The looting problem is no easier to deal with. Even in remote areas, most people know that pre-Columbian pieces fetch high prices in the great cities of the northern hemisphere. Especially to the indigent, the temptation to try and turn over a few dollars in this way must be very strong and will remain so as long as the trade endures. News of an ancient site is hard to keep secret, and here, for a change, is a cash crop whose harvest yields a good deal more than those that grow on trees or in the fields. Since life in the rural tropics of America can be far from easy, and sometimes very hard indeed, a moral lecture from a foreigner to the local looter is unlikely to do much good, although it has to be said that an astonishingly high proportion of local people will not touch the ruins, simply because they feel

it is wrong to do so. Impressive, too, is the dedication of the state-employed site guardians, who resist temptation and defy the predators, sometimes at the risk of their lives.

The scale of illegal damage ranges from scuffling about for chance surface finds to the most destructive open-cast mining of entire groups of buildings, in search of tombs among the masonry. Clandestine removal from the locality and from the country is carefully organized, with a chain of agents leading to the famous salerooms of the north. Until the very end of the chain, where people earn their living by their erudition in these matters, there is probably very little

Seibal
Structure A-1

Stanhopea sp.

appreciation of the importance of the traded pieces nor of the injury caused by their theft. Apart from the simple loss, each thing found at a site may be a clue to the significance of everything else there. This is especially so when a piece is inscribed with hieroglyphics. Some of the most poignant damage occurs with the large carved monoliths: stonecutting chainsaws are used to cut the texts into portable sections, which are then separated from their origins without record, probably for ever. Even worse, if possible, is the savage procedure of lighting a fire beside some great sculpture, then throwing water on the stone to burst it into fragments, in the hope that some of them will be both portable and saleable.

Clearly this is a matter for international accord, and several useful conventions are already in force. In the Maya countries, all ancient artefacts are required to be registered with the state and their export is forbidden. Old collections can present difficulties, but it is not reasonable to make them an exception. The real focus of the matter must be the transaction at the end of the chain, when the highest price is paid for an object before it disappears into a private museum, where, because of its illegality, it will remain out of the reach of scholars. By that stage, the piece will have been passed from hand to hand with such tact that its provenance and date of discovery are matters of only the vaguest conjecture, and its stature as a work of art exaggerated by successive vendors at the expense of its archæological significance. Clandestine sales can only be interrupted after expensive detective work, but those public dealers in these items who defy the law are surely within the reach of international pressure and legislation. Most urgently needed is a scheme for freezing the movement of any suspicious object until the vendor has satisfied all reasonable inquiries by the archæological institutions of the countries of origin.

What a difference there is between the illegal collector's provider and the Canadian archæologist who wrote at Monte Albán: 'Tearing them [grave goods] from their resting place was a cruel act: the cause of science and the pleasure we get from looking at them justify us only partly in breaking into these tombs.' One might add that in this unscrupulous age, the best protection for a site and its contents is never to be found at all.

Seibal lies in the depths of the Petén, on a bend of the Río de la Pasión. The main temple, known as Structure A-1, is not large, but is surrounded by four fine stelæ. These are well preserved due to the hardness of the stone, and bear dates from the latter half of the ninth century AD. A strong Teotihuacan influence can be seen in the carvings. Some distance away there are various other stelæ and an unusual round temple-base.

Sketch of stela at Seibal

THE FOREST SITE OF YAXCHILÁN

To get to Yaxchilán the visitor descends the Usumacinta river in a boat from a small frontier town upstream. Knowing that the site extends for at least a mile along the left bank of the river, he keenly scans the forest edge for signs of Lost Worlds. But no clue is to be seen, no surface of dressed stone catching the sunlight behind a screen of leaves, no line of wall or terrace. There is a faint suggestion of unnatural straightness in the last reach of the river before the landing, but it might just as well be a geological accident.

Only on coming to land and climbing twenty feet up the steep bank into the forest does the traveller find himself suddenly amongst the ruins, and in the strangest ambience. It is as though he were under the sea in some weed-infested Atlantis: the terraced complexities of temples, stairways and standing stones come to his notice one by one in a green dimness, dwarfed by the titanic growth of the forest. Only rarely do slanting rays of sunlight pierce the dense shade, striking sparsely down through the haphazard aisles of tree trunks, the scarce patches of brightness animated by hovering butterflies.

Trees a hundred and fifty feet high have rooted themselves in earth and ruins alike, as if the crumbling masonry had never had an independent purpose of its own. Giant stems rise through a tangle of lesser growth: leafage hangs in swags and clusters at every level, while vines of a prodigious luxuriance connect tree with tree. Everything on the jungle floor – stones, earth, ruins, fallen timber – is smothered with creepers, mosses and orchids.

So overwhelmed are these relics of the Maya that their existence in the remote past is almost impossible to visualize. The voice of history is muffled, like the legendary bells of sunken churches, whose tolling comes uncertainly through the swaying tides.

Going forward among the buildings and the stelæ which stand or lie in what were once wide ceremonial courts paved with sparkling stucco, the visitor soon perceives that the artistic achievement of this great city was quite outstanding. Energetic invention and sculptural skill are manifest in every monument. The subjects of the carvings fill their appointed places with an elegant assurance reminiscent of the great periods of Chinese art. At Yaxchilán the large hieroglyphic compositions under the soffits of the doorways, where mosses cannot thrive, are in a particularly fine state of preservation and must be among the greatest relief sculptures in the world.[1]

On the stelæ, the portrait figures show a matchless stateliness. Seeing traces of strongly tinted stucco one wonders what colour could have added to an already generous effect. Even now, after centuries of erosion and decay, the

YAXCHILÁN
Stela 1 and Great Court

Heliconia sp.

effigies almost breathe. Great lords are shown receiving the pleas of deferential fief-holders and bound captives; sacrifices are illustrated in touching progress. On the whole, the lords and the fief-holders look rather disagreeable, while the captives seem to be rendered with a surprising sympathy and kindness. The limbs of the latter, being more nearly naked, give greater scope for sculptural expression, but all the same the beholder is left wondering whether he sees the pathos of greatness brought low, in the shape of defeated enemies stripped of their dignity, or whether he sees the beginnings of libertarian feelings in a serfdom exasperated by centuries of oppression.

At the swift close of the tropical afternoon, with scarcely half an hour between full daylight and darkness, the natural world overtakes Yaxchilán with a vengeance. The monuments seem to sink back into the trees, while the noises of the forest crowd upon the ear. As dusk deepens, the cries of homing parrots and toucans give way to the tremendous nocturnal din of howler monkeys, which will boom and roar from the far bank of the Usumacinta in crescendos and rallentandos until dawn, interrupted only by the occasional great cough of a jungle cat. Rare shafts of moonlight slant down through the forest roof but now they show nothing but rampant vegetation: old and new civilizations are equally lost.

---

1. *Several of the Yaxchilán lintels were removed from the site and now repose in various major museums. Considering how sought after such beautiful things are by collectors and how unscrupulous have been looters over the years, we probably owe to this intervention their preservation and the decipherment of their hieroglyphs.*

THE ESCARPMENT SITE OF PALENQUE

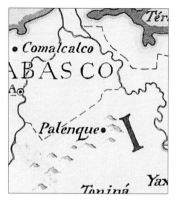

As an archæological site, Palenque stretches for seven miles along its wooded escarpment, but the most famous and important part stands on a high plateau only some twenty-five acres in extent, where the river Otolum levels out for a few hundred yards between cataracts. A tradition of embattlement accords well with formidable natural defences and visitors have always had to approach by steep ways, the surrounding slopes being precipitous beyond any possibility of cultivation. The outlook is entirely northward but most of the buildings stand far enough out from the mountainside to avoid being gloomy. High above the fertile plains, the situation of Palenque makes it a place of the spirit.

There are several major temple pyramids, some not yet fully explored. A number of them are relatively small, surmounted by buildings with the look of oratories. The most extensive construction is called the Palace, an assemblage of cloistered courtyards with a look-out tower.

The special character of the Palenque buildings derives from the peculiar shape of the roofs, best described as mansard, i.e. having two slopes to each face, the lower one steeper than the upper one. The eaves project boldly and some of the ridges still carry elaborate pierced roof-combs. A particularly elegant and complete example of the latter rises from the roof of the Temple of the Sun..

The important buildings at Palenque were adorned with fine sculpture in plaster: human figures, mythical creatures, stylized plants and panels of hieroglyphics, all in a crisp style of surpassing elegance. The designs have an assured fluency, reminiscent of baroque work in Europe. Sadly, the greater part of this enormous opus has perished, although enough remains to show the accomplishment in this medium of the Palenque Maya. The method was to construct the work in layers. The figures of humans and animals were built up on stone keys projecting from the wall; their clothes and ornaments were then modelled on top. Neither the exact style nor the technique were practised so successfully elsewhere.

More durable than the plaster is the carved stonework. The illustration shows two rows of archaic figures, considered to be the oldest large carvings at Palenque, and representing captives of some importance. They are forceful in execution, even primitive, unlike the majority of stone sculpture at the site, which is in a later mode and nearer in style to the plasterwork. The most graceful pieces are the interior panels of the temples. Made from a fine cream-coloured limestone, they are composed with a faultless elegance. They generally include lengthy hieroglyphic texts.

Palenque can be extraordinarily peaceful, with no other sounds than those of the birds, the river and the wind. Tranquillity, even if rarer than formerly, is still the essence of the place, when the courts of the palace bask in the sunshine, and the quietness is accented by the slight movements of tiny butterflies.

PALENQUE
Courtyard in the Palace

A Remarkable Burial

The huge majority of mankind has left no trace for posterity: burials beyond numbering are swallowed by the earth and an infinity of bodies is gone to nourish other forms of life. Most attempts to defend venerable human remains from the rust of time come to nothing in the end, so that the unbroken tombs which do survive are rare, remarkable and often moving.

In the Maya area, almost all socially important burials are found in the masonry of temples, generally under or near the stairways. This having become generally known, many fine buildings have been irretrievably damaged by looters searching for graves and the ancient offerings they might contain.

It would be tedious to catalogue all the things which might be found with the remains of an eminent personage: more interesting, perhaps, would be an account of the most astonishing tomb ever found in the Maya area.

For some time the Temple of the Inscriptions at Palenque had aroused the curiosity of scholars. In the temple which stands on its summit, some of the paving stones were seen to be provided with round holes inlaid with accurately fitted stone plugs. In 1949 the Mexican archæologist Alberto Ruz noticed that the walls of the temple did not rest on the floor, but continued some way below the pavement, indicating that there might be a cavity beneath. Excavation followed, disclosing first a vault, and then a stairway leading down into the heart of the pyramid. This steep tunnel was entirely blocked with stones and earth, and four seasons of work were needed before the bottom end was reached.

There the investigators discovered a rough wall with a chest in front of it, containing sea-shells filled with red pigment (the colour of mourning), jade objects, earthenware dishes and a pearl. A short distance behind this barrier was another low wall, which had sealed the passage into a tomb for five or six young people. Into one side of the vault of this passage was set a finely worked triangular stone. This was carefully removed in June 1952, disclosing a large and magnificent crypt, twenty-nine feet long, thirteen feet wide and twenty-three feet from the floor to the cap-stone of the vault.

Round the walls of the chamber were nine plaster relief figures, richly attired and believed to be the *Bolonti-Kiú,* the nine Lords of the Night and of the nine layers of the underworld. A large sarcophagus stood in the centre of the floor, resting on six stone pillars and covered by a beautifully sculpted rectangular lid of dolomitic limestone, nine inches thick. The quality of the sculpture and of the architecture itself was immediately seen to be spectacular; further inspection revealed that everything in the burial was the best of which the Classic Maya were capable.

Below the carved lid, which bore two dates, AD 683 and 692, was a plain

Stelæ at Calakmul

interior lid, also of stone. Under that reposed the skeleton of a tall man, forty
or fifty years old at his death. The sides and bottom of the coffin were painted
red, as had been a shroud, rotted long ago to dust but which had left its pigment
on the bones beneath. The body had been attired in a jade regalia: a head-dress,
a jade mosaic mask, necklaces, a pectoral, bracelets, rings (one for each finger
of both hands) and ear-rings, with huge artificial pearls made of mother-of-
pearl pieces glued together. In addition, the mouth and both hands had each
held a great jade bead, and two jade figures lay nearby. Yet more jade, in the
form of a ceremonial belt, had been found on the lid of the sarcophagus.

Under the stone coffin, on the floor, were various ceramic jars and plates,
originally filled with food and drink for the dead man on the day of his
funeral. In the same place were two beautifully modelled plaster heads,
evidently broken from complete figures which must be either destroyed or
elsewhere. Indeed, one of the broken plaster relief figures in the Palacio
appears to be the source of one of these buried heads.

In spite of the fact that this burial was defended by the rubble in the stairway
and the walls outside the crypt, it was joined to the sanctuary (eighty-two feet
above) by a mystic connection, put there to link the dead dignitary in his tomb
with the living worshippers in the temple above. This was the effigy of a serpent.
Springing from the sarcophagus as a plaster model, its form changed to a hollow
moulding in the stone as it ascended the steps of the stairway, until it ended
under those paving stones with holes in them, where the excavations had started.

This extraordinary grave was treated throughout its excavation with reverence.
The general solemnity was an impressive token of the respect felt by most
Mexicans for their pre-Hispanic predecessors, especially those unearthed in the
cause of science. When the archæological investigations were complete, the
replacement of the human remains in the tomb was done as a quiet ceremony, and
the chamber then closed with a grille, to prevent too near an approach by visitors.

THE FAUNA OF THE MAYA AREA

The fauna of the Maya area is especially rich in its number of species. This is due to the fact that many types of bird and animal have converged on Central America and Mexico, after developing separately in North and South America. Several ecological niches have thus come to be filled twice over. For instance, the jaguar (*Felis onca*) extended its habitat to Central America from South America, while the mountain lion or puma (*F. concolor*) is from the North. There are two distinct sorts of deer, the principal northern one being the white-tailed deer (*Odocoileus virginianus*) which is common in the United States of America, and the southern representative being the brocket (*Mazama americana*). And so it is with wild pigs, monkeys, rodents, various small carnivores and many of the birds.

Numerous though the species may be, many are becoming rare because of pursuit by man. Laws exist to protect the more vulnerable creatures, but enforcement is difficult in an extensive and sparsely populated terrain. Except in the national parks and archæological zones, state vigilance is impossible. The only hope of maintaining stocks of the rarer species is through education.

Tuxtla Gutiérrez Zoological Park is doing fine work in this regard, and is setting an example to similar institutions. Originally, the zoo occupied a site in the city, which is the capital of Chiapas, and had many exotic species among its exhibits. However, it eventually became very run down; and when a decision was made to move, the then Director[1] was able to plan the present establishment from its inception. The new collection was sensibly restricted to the larger fauna of the State of Chiapas, which in fact meant the inclusion of all the more noticeable animals, birds and reptiles which occur in the whole Maya area. Concentrating on this large but entirely possible field, the enterprise is a great success, with surprisingly few omissions.

The site chosen is a thickly wooded mountainside south of the city. As much forest as possible has been left standing, and some of the enclosures are so large that on looking into them one has the impression that they must go back for miles. Indeed, it is possible for most of the occupants to hide completely if they feel so inclined. Each animal enclosure has a stream running through it, usually with a waterfall. There are several enormous bird cages, and some of the birds and smaller animals are not confined at all, being kept on the premises by feeding.

The pleasure and instruction given by this place to its visitors must be worth every peso spent on it. The natural circumstances of the various species, including the dangers in which they currently find themselves, are clearly stated on notice-boards, and there is a general message to all, to take more care than heretofore of the non-human occupants of the tropics.

White-tailed Deer
(*Odocoileus virginianus*)

The Classic period Temple of the Jaguars is some way apart from the rest of the excavated buildings at Palenque. It stands on a steep hillside, and the front part has collapsed due to a landslide, and probably also due to rough treatment in 1832 by Count Maximilian de Waldeck, who tried to remove the temple's stucco inscriptions but succeeded only in breaking them.

1. *Doctor Álvarez del Toro.*

PALENQUE – *Temple of the Jaguars*

THE ISLAND SITE OF TOPOXTE

Topoxte is an island at the west end of Lake Yaxhá, one of a series of lagoons stretching across the middle of the Petén department of northern Guatemala. The ancient settlement extends to one or two adjacent islets and must have been sited on the lake for security. Its occupation was not a long one by comparison with Classic sites such as the enormous metropolis of Yaxhá, only a mile or two away on the north shore: Topoxte was founded about AD 1250 and abandoned by the end of the fifteenth century.

The site demonstrates the circular progress of the centre of Maya culture. It will be remembered that at the close of the Preclassic the focus of artistic activity and temporal power moved northwards from the highlands into the rain forests, where it remained for several centuries before following its own previous influence into the Yucatán peninsula. Around the tenth century AD, the Yucatán was settled by peoples from central Mexico, such as the Toltec and the Xiú (who took over Chichén Itzá and Uxmal respectively). In due course the purely Maya people known as the Itzá took themselves off to the south, and established themselves back in the rain forest zone, at places such as Topoxte.

As elsewhere, the ordinary citizens of Topoxte seem to have been the same stock throughout their history. Only the governing classes came and went, and one imagines that a return to feudalism would only have been tolerable to the locals in return for organization and protection unavailable from their own resources. This supposition is borne out by the defensive nature of the site. The actions of the Classic rulers of Yaxhá must surely have been remembered by the populace, perhaps with some rancour, and the Itzá presumably owed their acceptance as overlords to the turbulence and uncertainty of the times.

The Topoxte buildings show various features invented in the Yucatán, notably the angular arrangement of surfaces on the temple pyramids and the use of beamed-roof construction in assembly rooms. In common with all Postclassic sites, the standard of architecture is not very high: the buildings are all ruinous and the main interest of Topoxte lies in its character as an island fortress.

One curious feature, unique indeed, is a series of miniature stelæ. They stand no higher out of the ground than mile-stones on an English roadside and are completely plain except for holes drilled apparently at random on the front surfaces. In fact, they were almost certainly plastered and adorned with paintings at the time of their dedication, and the holes could well have held inlay of shell or jade.

TOPOXTE
Principal Temple

Overgrown altar at Yaxhá

OBSERVATIONS ON THE BUILDINGS AT TIKAL

Tikal is one of the best documented archæological sites in Latin America. It is also one of the most visually impressive. The ruins are in the middle of the Petén rain forest, a region which contains many ancient Maya centres. Uaxactún is only a few miles to the north; El Mirador, Nakum, Yaxhá and Río Azul are not far away. The nearest modern town, Flores, in Lake Petén, is the site of Tayasal, former island stronghold of the Itzá.

Five spectacularly tall pyramidal structures survive at Tikal, their elaborate roof ornaments and temple portals rising clear above the highest treetops. Hidden in the forest below are a great many other stone buildings of varying size and importance, but all forming part of this ceremonial centre. The remains of humbler edifices extend for over a mile in every direction, mainly houses raised on low mounds to prevent flooding in the seasonal rains and much the same as those built by the Maya today.

As the mapping of Tikal has been comprehensive, the geometry of the architecture can be considered with some ease. The salient features, so far as technique goes, are long and accurate straight lines of masonry, confident corbel-vaulting, perfect verticals and horizontals, symmetrical front elevations and a conscientious use of several highly effective canons of proportion. Less obvious to the casual beholder, but evident all too soon to the artist, is the fact that the corners of most of the principal buildings are not exact right angles. Drawing any temple, one's paper is soon peppered with vanishing points; while working them all out, there is time to reflect that surely this cannot have been due to incompetence. After all, the Maya were gifted mathematicians as well as precise observers of the visible universe and its movements. The patiently achieved accuracy of their astronomy, and the fact that it is hard to find corrected faults in their sculpture, lead one to think that the corners of their pyramids and terraces were deliberately made less or more than ninety degrees. They permitted themselves a common alignment for a group or complex of buildings, generally based on some periodic conjunction in the heavens, but there was clearly an inhibition when it came laying out the individual buildings.

We already know – and the knowledge is reinforced from time to time by fresh interpretations of the Maya texts – that the cardinal directions were deified and revered. Each had various properties and was allotted a distinct and significant colour, white for north, red for east, yellow for south and black for west. The Postclassic Maya liturgies, recorded in detail by the early Spanish chroniclers, involved numerous devotions addressed to these directions or to the gods in charge of them, and one supposes that this cult existed in Classic times. It seems reasonable to deduce that laying out a temple pyramid rectangularly was thought to be a solecism. Designing the monuments with the sides *all* askew, as they are at Tikal, is really quite an achievement, far more difficult than doing it with all the angles square.

It has been suggested that the centres of all the major sites were huge observatories, that the haphazard-looking elements in the layouts were carefully considered in every detail rather than allowed to develop accidentally. This is hard to prove, however, with over two thousand distinct stars visible to the naked eye on a clear night: an enthusiast for alignments of architecture with stars could find an astral counterpart for practically any terrestrial line. It seems more likely that some sort of divination was practised during the siting and construction of every separate building, with, however, particular regard to one major alignment at each site. It is known that certain alignments previously in use in Central Mexico appeared in the north of the Maya area with the arrival of the Toltecs.

TIKAL – Temples II, III & IV seen from Temple I

TIKAL
View from Temple V

New Names for
Old Buildings

Nomenclature is difficult to get right. Those who have to label the buildings do not want to be too dry, but feel on the other hand that they should not be unduly romantic. 'Temple of the Round Altars' *does* sound more alluring than 'Structure B-4', but often there is nothing much to distinguish a particular heap of ruined masonry before it has been excavated, and B-4 does very well to be going on with. Even if the building subsequently turns out to be exceptional, by then the dull name may have become so well used that it cannot be changed. The largest temple pyramids at Tikal, among the most astonishing monuments in the world, are simply and sensibly numbered one to five.

As far as names implying use goes, the temples are the easiest to deal with: imposing religious structures with obvious sanctuaries, the use proposed for them is clearly correct. Less satisfactory is the naming of those complicated ranges of buildings in the vicinity of the temples, variously called palaces, nunneries and monasteries. The use of these apartments is still a matter of guessing, but they are most likely to have been residences for priests and others, perhaps used temporarily at times of special religious observance. Fasting and general abstinence were an important part of Maya devotions, and priestly celebrants may have lived apart in these places in the days leading up to important ceremonies. Another possible group of occupants might have been their occasional but much-honoured human sacrifices. There is no particular evidence in favour of habitation by copiously attended royal families or by permanent communities vowed to celibacy.

Buildings are often named from architectural or decorative features, like the Pyramid of Five Terraces at Etzná or the Platform of Eagles and Jaguars at Chichén. This is a good idea, except where the chosen name has some extraneous association, like the Iglesia (church, which it never was) at Chichén or the Temple of the Cross at Palenque, which inevitably conjures up the nineteenth-century red herring of Christianity having somehow found its way to the Americas during the Classic period. Similarly, the various 'castles', like the Castillo at Chichén, are misleadingly named. One or two fortress sites exist, but no castles, Maya warfare being a matter of raids and brisk encounters: long drawn-out defence was a notion they were not obliged to absorb until set upon by the Europeans in the sixteenth century.

A further problem is what to call the places themselves. The peculiarly arid word 'site' is in constant use, largely because these great settlements are unlike anything elsewhere, the nearest comparison being the polities of the Khmer in Asia. Tikal, Copán and others have been called cities, but that seems to imply a greater concentration of people than the Maya were used to. Even in the most important places, ordinary dwellings were dispersed over a wide area, with the central groupings of devotional buildings not inhabited by ordinary families at all. 'Ceremonial centre', admittedly another hideous expression, is probably the best term to suggest a religious nucleus in a secular community.

Temple V, Tikal
from the N

Top of Temple V

FINDINGS AT ALTUN HÁ

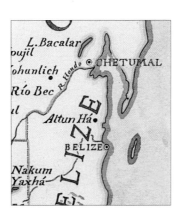

The archæological investigation of Altun Há began in competition with looters and vandals who had been digging among the ruins for grave goods over many years, with the result that several buildings had been demolished beyond rescue. However, the Government of Belize and the Royal Ontario Museum took over and have uncovered and protected a large part of the site. There have been some spectacular finds, and research at Altun Há has had valuable implications for a wide area.

Although the name is a modern one, a translation into Maya of Rockstone Pond, the nearest Creole village, the archæological site is probably extremely ancient. It is now thought, largely from other finds in Belize, that the ancestors of the Classic Maya were in the same part of the world as early as 10,000 BC. While the primitive inhabitants of Altun Há left little of an enduring nature, the artificially enlarged lagoon at the south end of the site points to an early occupation.

The first datable finds relate to the Preclassic, when the pace of development began to accelerate. The earliest surviving buildings are from towards the close of that period, the principal one being a pyramid beside the reservoir just mentioned. Today this building is no more than a heap of debris, but it was originally as tall as the pyramid in the illustration, which is known as Structure B-4.

Altun Há was culturally at its most active in the early and middle Classic. Its people established a well-served cult of the Sun God, Kinich Ahau, with whom Structure B-4 is strongly associated.

B-4 is now revealed in its second distinguishable phase of construction, dated AD 600-650. As usual, earlier stages were buried under later ones. Six stages later than the one we now see have been cleared away: they were relatively minor additions to the structure and when found were all very partial and mixed up with each other in their decay. The edifice is notable for having had round altars on its successive summits, the surviving one of which was overlaid with others, now removed. Rebuilding of the temple being in the nature of a ritual sepulture of the previous one, various offerings were buried with the old altars. In the case of the altar now exposed at the top of the building, a rich sacrificial collection of ornaments, many of them jade and deliberately broken, was burnt and then buried in a mass of red pigment, so that the find was fittingly described as 'a fossilized ceremony'.[1] As has been said, red was the Maya colour of mourning.

Just as exciting was the disclosure of a magnificent human burial inside the rectangular block of masonry between the two stairheads at the top of the building. Here, to judge by his grave-goods, lay a priest of the Sun God. The

ALTUN HÁ
Structure B-4

outstanding offering in the tomb was a massive translucent stone head of that deity: six inches high and weighing nearly ten pounds, it is one of the largest carved pieces of jade ever found in America. Also in the burial were several eccentric flints, pressure-flaked into strange silhouettes, and certain terracotta incense-burners, covered with moulded spines and peculiar to this site.

Another most unusual object was unearthed at Altun Há: a gold and copper alloy pendant imported from the Panama region before the end of the sixth century AD. Apart from this one object, worked metal is unknown in the Maya area until the Postclassic.

From the close of the seventh century, the standards of construction at Altun Há declined; and in about AD 900 its rulers either abandoned it or were evicted by their erstwhile subjects. Deliberate desecration of tombs and temples gives evidence of some violence at this juncture, but the crisis does not appear to have been accompanied by famine, invasion or disease. The ordinary people of Altun Há continued to occupy the same place throughout the Postclassic, but without the elaborate ceremonies and theocratic organization of former times.

---

1. *David M. Pendergast, Royal Ontario Museum.*

HORMIGUERO
Structure 2

THE CONSERVATION
OF HORMIGUERO

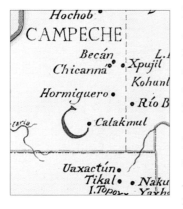

Hormiguero is in the south-east corner of the Mexican state of Campeche, about twenty-five miles south-west of Xpujil. It was clearly a major ceremonial centre in Classic times and its recent exploration will doubtless yield all manner of interesting information.

In 1984 the site, whose name means an ant-heap, was swarming with appropriate activity. A team of experts from the Mexican Institute of Anthropology and History was busily investigating the central buildings, supervising restoration work and exploring the peripheral structures. About fifty people were employed: the village of Xpujil provided the less skilled labour while the masons all came from Oxkutzkab, a town over a hundred miles away in the state of Yucatán and famed throughout Mexico for this particular craft.

The biggest surviving structure at Hormiguero is based on a large terrace, so that the walls themselves begin some twenty feet above the original forest floor. Steep twin towers flank a wide central frontage of typical Río Bec design, in the middle of which is a doorway formed as a gigantic fanged mouth. During repairs the workmen passed ceaselessly through this portal, in with empty barrows or loads of lime mortar for the plasterers and masons, and out carrying rubble. The façade was approached from wooden scaffolding and rough ladders, all made of poles cut near the site and held together with rope. There were no machines and minimal noise – just the clink and scrape of picks and shovels, and the sound of human voices.

The programme started with clearing the forest from the general area, then mapping the structures disclosed and finally attending to the decayed buildings. These had to be carefully freed from rubble and plants before restoration could be attempted. An important task was saving cut stones from the débris and ascertaining their original place in the building. In these forest sites some huge tree is frequently found not only to have forced a building apart, but also to be then holding it

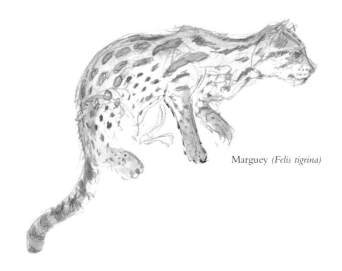

Marguey *(Felis tigrina)*

together. Just as common is a Laocoönesque entanglement, where a tree has run riot in a wall and then sent down a creeper from high in its branches to engulf the disordered stones below in a network of roots so complicated that the lines of the original masonry can hardly be traced. All kinds of props and artifices must be employed in the disentangling, and often a tree-stump has to be left *in situ*.

With any particular building the policy of the Institute is to restore every element for which the original stones can be found. To this objective is sensibly added the reconstruction, using suitable stone, of indisputable and large components such as terraces and stairways, whose layout can reasonably be inferred from the remainder of the structure. The repetitive and symmetrical nature of much of the ornament enables the workmen to make good sense out of some very badly damaged features, although they have to be constantly on the look-out for asymmetry in the original design. Sculpture in stone is difficult and expensive, and in any case it is considered incorrect to insert new pieces into a monument without very good reason (generally structural). The masons are more or less restricted to stone-cutting as opposed to sculpture, and putting the stonework together from its old components. When a building has been mended to the limits set by this policy, it has to be left in such a state that it will not be unnecessarily vulnerable. This is principally a matter of leaving no crevices on the upper surfaces where plants can lodge and begin their rapid growth into large and destructive trees.

The protection of plasterwork is a special problem. Originally the panels of relief ornament in plaster were defended from the tropical rain by projecting ledges and cornices. If these are completely missing from a building, as is often the case, they cannot be reconstructed by conjecture and so have to be left off. Although the exact ingredients for the original plaster are not known (the recipe in the Valley of Mexico is supposed to have been lime and crushed sea-shells mixed with the juice of a cactus called *nopal*), the only practical scheme is to try to imitate the appearance and qualities of the old materials, using the toughest possible modern lime plaster.

After the workmen leave a site, arrangements have to be made for the buildings to be kept clear of vegetation and policed against looters. These are not easy matters, especially in remote districts of thick forest, but they are being treated with increasing determination by all the governments in the Maya area.

Buzzards and vultures

91

Preservation versus Romanticism

For artists at least, the appeal of long-ruined buildings is a romantic one. The tragedies of downfall are softened by nature, the hard edges of violent destruction blunted by time. The lines of a building which was broken yesterday can be drawn for the most part with the edge of a ruler, but the architecture of long-desolate places is continually interrupted by the attrition of the elements, by the rampant growth of plants and by the ineluctable workings of gravity.

When approaching a ruin to draw it, it is hard to say how one would wish to find it. Even some very large Maya buildings, having decayed century by century under sun and rain and the exuberance of tropical vegetation, are scarcely recognizable as coming from the hand of man. For instance, a stranger walking or rather pushing and cutting his way through the enormous site of Yaxhá in northern Guatemala before it was partially cleared, would have needed expert knowledge to realize that he was amongst artificial hills rather than natural ones. Even a superficial survey requires the removal of vegetation and fallen rubble to reveal the structures beneath.

Nowadays the most cursory exploration is usually sufficient to commit a national government to protect a site of any importance. Repairs must then be undertaken, lintels and vaults strengthened, sometimes only just in time to prevent a collapse. Such fallen stones as can be recognized as belonging to particular places above can be re-embedded, the broken plasterwork can be patched up and the whole structure defended in some measure against weather and weeds by skilful pointing of the masonry.

These works leave the buildings looking very bleak, and the fresh mortar glares so much in the sunlight that it is hard to discern the modelling of stones and plaster or properly to appreciate the more delicate intervals of the architecture. Most of the original plaster coating of the buildings is usually missing, and repairs to the underlying structure make it look particularly unfinished. However, only a few years are required to mellow these raw terraces and walls, and to convert a place of modern invasion back to a romantic and numinous ruin. A few weeds, hardly worth eradicating, soon appear in remote corners of the masonry; bees and wasps and swallows build their nests, while a feeling of imperturbable antiquity descends. A watchman keeps an eye on things, checking the everlasting aggressions of the vegetation, cutting orchids and cactuses out of the roof-combs before they become big enough to dislodge stones, and with his presence (and the law behind him) discouraging the attentions of looters and vandals.

Río Bec
Temple B

However, even this small vigilance can prove costly: Central America and Mexico are full of ruins which received state-provided attention at the time of their discovery, but which have had to be abandoned since for lack of funds. Uaxactún is a notable example: extensive work and research were done there in the 1930s but it proved too difficult to staff and maintain the site later on. Early in the 1970s it would have been quite impossible to draw any major structure without clearing half an acre of trees, and hardly a soul in the neighbouring village knew the whereabouts of more than three of the monuments. In fact Uaxactún has now come into a new era of care from the government, but reabandonment of any but the most frequented sites is always a possibility, archæological importance notwithstanding. The visiting artist is advised to make hay while the sun shines, even if he finds conditions only just good enough for him to get on with his work.

The scholarly explorer Raymond Merwin, working for the Peabody Museum, found the site of Río Bec in 1910, and carried out a survey. Nevertheless, subsequent visiting archæologists were quite unable to locate this lovely temple until its rediscovery in 1974. It stands in thick forest on the Campeche/Quintana Roó border, about twenty-five miles south of the new road between Chetumal and Francisco Escárcega. The site has given its name to the architecture of the area, which is described in the essay on Xpujil.

MUTILATIONS

It always seems rather depraved to derange human features so as to achieve an artificial canon of beauty, but distortions and mutilations of this kind crop up all over the world, most of them without the slightest pretext of physical improvement, from stretched necks in Africa to compressed feet in China.

The Maya induced in their children a number of physical deformities which would generate a good deal of worry nowadays if suspected of having occurred naturally.

A flattened forehead was considered a lovely thing, and was achieved by pressing the heads of very young babies between boards. This custom pertained to all classes and when in the sixteenth century the Maya were asked why they did it, they explained 'the custom gives us a noble air and moreover our heads are thus better adapted to carry loads'. There is no evidence that this curious usage damaged the little creatures' brains, and one assumes that it was not painful, the Maya being extremely kind towards their children. Skulls have been found in which the deformity is quite astonishingly marked, in old and evidently very distinguished people, to judge by the richness of their burials. One may conclude, therefore, that the practice did no great harm and did not shorten peoples' lives. It is also seen in artistic representations of lowlier folk. Bishop Landa's account of the Maya gives the impression that in his day this artificial deformity was virtually universal.

Whether the head-flattening helped or not, it is worth noting that the ancient Maya were indeed accustomed to carrying heavy loads – eighty pounds was quite normal – over long distances, the weight distributed between their backs and their foreheads by means of a cloth or fibre band. Incidentally, the Arawaks and Caribs of the Antilles, who colonised their islands from South America, did the same thing to the heads of their children, saying that it toughened their skulls against the blows of their enemies. When it came to heads, in one sense the ancient Maya did know what they were about since they were prepared to attempt trepanation, that is to say

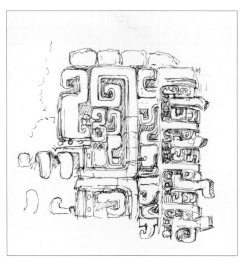

Corner of Structure 1 at Chicanná

96

CHICANNÁ
Structure 2

King vulture *(Sarcorhamphus papa)* and opposite

cutting a piece out of a person's cranium in order to relieve some ailment inside. While it is not known if these operations had the desired effect, it does seem likely, for many of the trepanned skulls found in burials show signs of healing before death.

Strabismus (squint) was another common deformity. Bishop Landa records in his account of the Yucatec Maya that the mothers would dangle a bead over their offsprings' noses, or tie a little lump of pitch to their hair in front, so as to make them look inwards at it.

Less severe, and restricted to important people, teeth were drilled in front and then inlaid with jade or turquoise pieces to fill the holes. The teeth of humbler persons were filed in a saw pattern, this office being performed by old women. Ears were pierced for ear-plugs, and the septums of noses for nose-plugs, as can be seen from practically every stela showing a ruler. The best ear-plugs were made of jade, and many fine examples survive, some of them extremely large and involving grotesque distortion of the wearer's ear lobes.

Chicanná is beside the road from Chetumal to Francisco Escárcega, a mile or so west of Becán. There are several fine buildings, with unusually well-bonded masonry. The Mexican government recently undertook a large programme of restoration at the site.

A THEATRICAL ARCHITECTURE

The architecture of Xpujil is intended to astonish, in which it succeeds to admiration. Viewed from afar, the main structure appears as three tall towers, with stairways of an improbable steepness leading to temples on top. The remains of gigantic masks adorn the flights of steps, which on a nearer approach turn out to be almost vertical and quite unclimbable. Indeed, they lead to nothing, as the temples on top are no more than façades with false doorways. All in all, it is a case of maximum effect from minimum effort, a most stylish affair.

The stone used in the building of Xpujil gave a good key to the covering coats of stucco, much of which has therefore survived. As elsewhere in the Maya realm, the temple buildings were originally coloured: all that remains now is white plaster and bare stone, and the whole edifice is so light in tone that it catches the eye from a great way off, sparkling in the sun above the treetops, or standing up from the horizon in strong relief against the grey storm-clouds of the rainy season.

The dramatic architectural manner of Xpujil is called Río Bec, from the name of another impressive site some twenty-five miles to the south (see pages 70-71). Scholars have described the style as decadent, with the suggestion that it might have been carried out more appropriately in theatrical cardboard. However, the craftsmanship is far from slipshod, the jointing of some of the stonework in this region being extremely fine: the Río Bec masons seem to have been practically alone in understanding the proper bonding of masonry, failures in this respect elsewhere having led to the premature dissolution of countless Maya buildings.

Sadly, the roof-combs which originally surmounted the towers at Xpujil are quite gone. They were probably as elaborate and as high as the builders dared to make them, and would have given the tallest tower a height above ground level of over eighty feet.

The stone at Xpujil was easy to work, but the corresponding disadvantage is that all the carved inscriptions have been eroded into illegibility. Not a single carved date survives, although other evidence shows that these buildings were finished in the seventh or eighth century AD.

XPUJIL
Structure 1

PEACE
AT BECÁN

As a rule, people who are afraid of the world around them suppose that there are angry gods, and if they can express their ideas successfully they raise images so terrifying and of such an implacable aspect that the terror continues even when for the time being nature seems benign. The horrid zoomorphic altars at Copán and Quiriguá exemplify this; and at most sites where detailed sculpture and carved texts have survived, images of death and the wrath of heaven are not far to seek. Since they occurred with great frequency in the inscriptions, the hieroglyphs dealing with doom and cataclysm were among the first non-numerate elements to be deciphered, and are therefore well recognized. With these prophetic utterances in stone, wood and plaster in such quantities about them, the generally gloomy drift must have been clear even to those Maya who were unable to read the texts, and the effect ominous and frightening. Few modern visitors would deny that a sense of omen survives palpably at the majority of Maya ruins.

How extraordinarily pleasant, then, to come upon a different atmosphere, as at Becán. It is quite a large site, but very decayed. The flat open spaces, once plastered, are grown over by grass and weeds, while the surrounding pyramids are covered with bushes and cactus or swallowed by the encroaching forest. Round the entire site runs a huge moat and rampart, with evidence that for centuries the people of the place were obliged to consider their defence. A set of extravagant triple towers in the grandiose style of Río Bec, complete with sham stairways and false sanctuaries, used to dominate the central space, but this edifice has long since rotted to a shapeless heap. What does remain, however, is one high terrace, quite complete and with an air of extraordinary grace. It encloses a little courtyard, perhaps once covered by a roof, and with a decorative scheme both charming and restrained. The main entrance is from the ceremonial stairway of the pyramid. Opposite, a central doorway leads up a couple of steps to a terrace, almost a balcony, which looks out northwards over the tree tops. Doors in the other two sides disclose small rooms. The court measures only ten yards by eleven and all its proportions are perfect: the principles of harmonic composition are demonstrated with elegance and simplicity, quite as well as in any classical building of similar scale in the Old World. The geometry of this structure must have given much pleasure to those who planned and built it and one hopes that its humanizing influence was felt by many succeeding generations.

Below the courtyard are various rooms connected by stairs inside the

Becán, Structure VIII before excavation

pyramid, one with a water-cistern and drains (a bathroom? a lavatory?). Odd little windows give on to the main open space of the site. There is a strong feeling of amenity as well as of ceremony.

As the neighbouring sites of Chicanná and Xpujil bristle with the heads of furious-looking sky-gods, we must suppose that Becán also had plenty of these and other symbols of divine wrath. Nevertheless, the only monument at Becán to survive in a nearly complete state gives an impression of gentleness, humanity and contentment.

(This piece was written before major restoration work in 1984.)

BECÁN
Structure 4

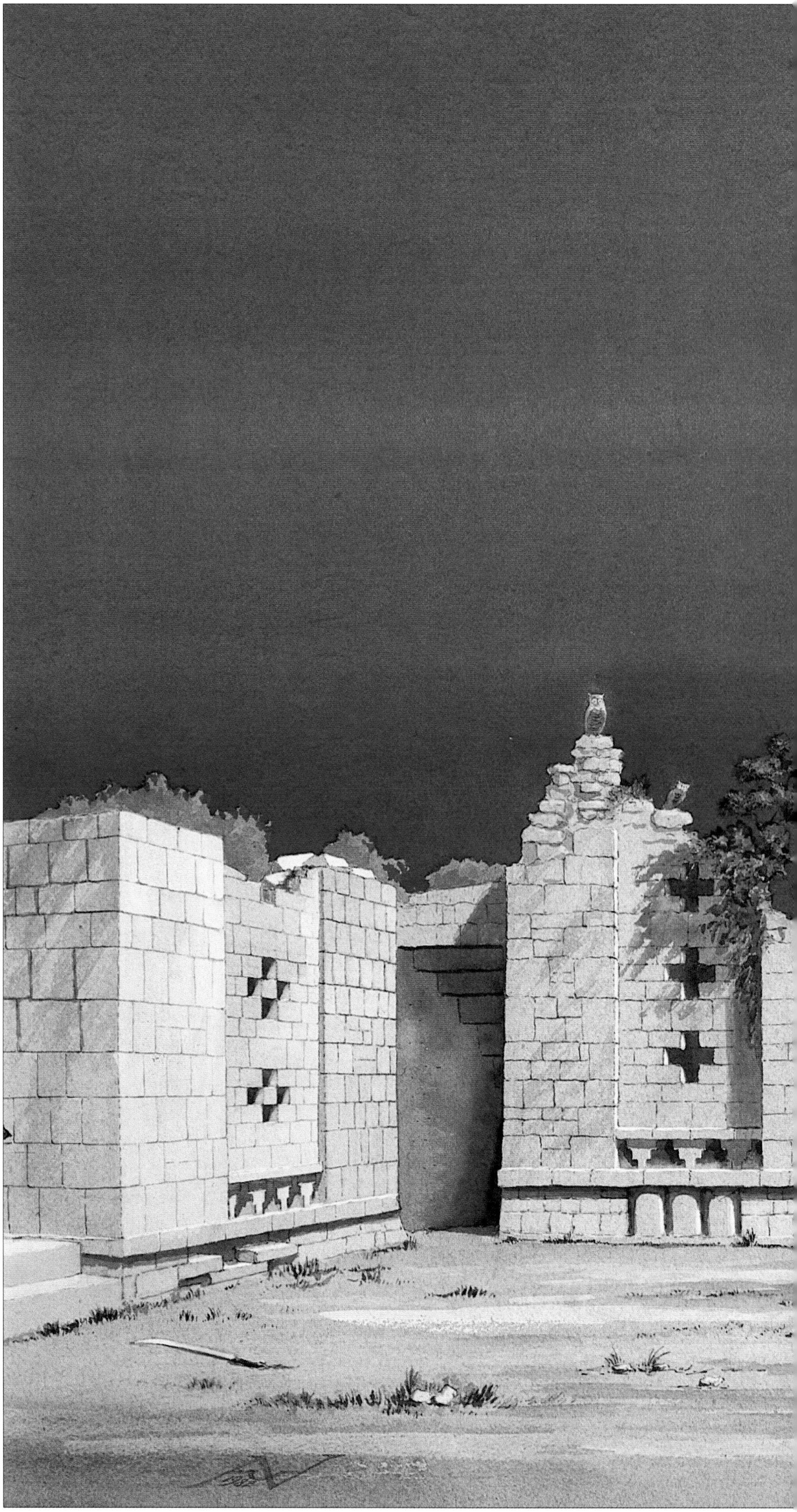

CUITLACOCHE

One wonders what the Classic Maya made of the fungus *cuitlacoche (Ustilago maydis)* or corn smut. Since it is a crop-reducing parasite of maize, which they had carefully bred over the centuries to give larger yields, it seems impossible that they would have treated it other than with total disapproval.

Cuitlacoche grows as a gall on maize ears, which in natural conditions are made especially receptive to it by damage from wind, hail or insects. The galls deform the maize ears to such an extent that the kernels are inedible. Losses from the fungus in Central America and Mexico frequently amount to 80% of the crop from the field in question. Apart from this, the galls have the tiresome property of becoming extremely combustible when dry and acting like tinder. They are, consequently, a notorious fire hazard during storage and at threshing time.

High losses from *cuitlacoche* in Mexico and further south are largely due to the growing of two successive crops in one year. Spores from the first crop infect the second, and spores from the latter lie dormant in the dry Mexican winter, until they can invade the first crop of the following year. The incidence of the disease is much increased by storm damage when the crop is coming into ear. The only satisfactory controls are by breaking the continuous succession of maize crops with a lapse of at least two years, and by breeding and sowing resistant varieties, principally ones with long husks, which make access by the spores more difficult.

Cuitlacoche

Although this does not have much bearing on Maya agriculture of a thousand years ago, it is interesting (and disquieting) that the fungus builds up a resistance to arsenical fungicides in a very short time. Add to this the fact that there are six billion spores in one cubic inch of *cuitlacoche*, and it will be seen as an organism with formidable powers of propagation and survival.

Further complications derive from the fact of *cuitlacoche* being used as a food. Although the infected kernels are nutritionally useless, the galls can be removed from the ears and cooked. They are considered a delicacy in certain quarters, even though they contain a number of alkaloids which can induce serious digestive troubles. It is not possible to tell if *cuitlacoche* was a favourite dish of the pre-hispanic Maya, but it was almost certainly known by

DZIBILNOCAC – *Structure A-1*

White-fronted Parrot *(Amazona albifrons)*

them to be edible. Today it appears on the vegetable stalls of Mexico, in spite of the fact that the only sensible thing to do with infected maize is to burn it, certainly not to keep it growing for a luxury market. It is often said that pre-Columbian Americans were unbalanced in certain matters, such as the proportion of the population employed in the construction of their monuments, and the huge sacrifices of the Aztecs; but one should not be too hard on them, looking from our own times with their vast horrors and dreadful political excesses. A foolish view of a crop disease, coupled perhaps to bad luck with the weather and an over-intensive system of agriculture, can do much damage today: it seems unlikely that the ancient Maya would have allowed their commonwealth to be threatened in such a way.

Of Dzibilnocac, all that could be seen in 1982 was a ruinous double-towered structure, whose more complete southern end is illustrated here. The Mexican government carried out restoration work at the site, two years after the picture was drawn.

AGRICULTURE

Ancient Maya agriculture was long thought to have been based on the extensive system known as *milpa* or swidden, whereby the aboriginal or primary (and when that ran out, secondary) vegetation was cut down and burnt, so that crops could be planted in its place. In the new fields thus obtained, natural fertility and freedom from weeds are both shortlived. Seven years is a long cropping period, while five or six are more usual. The *milpa* system is very widely operated throughout Latin America today and is certainly a most ancient practice. In terms of labour, and speaking very approximately, a man with help from his wife and children can cope with a plot large enough to feed an extended family of well over a dozen people (twenty-four has been given as a figure in the Yucatán) with occasional modest surpluses for trade. The timber felled in the clearances is not all wasted, and some trees are left standing and survive the burning, but since it takes centuries of non-disturbance for the vegetation to recover the stature of primary forest, the tree-covered areas are gradually reduced. Indeed, the more fertile areas, when cleared of trees, tend to revert to savannah if abandoned, so that primary tropical woodland once felled will never naturally recover its former extent. Since forest attracts and generates precipitation, its reduction also decreases rainfall, and if pursued excessively will change the climate over a wide area, with poor prospects for any kind of farming. This is seen to be happening to a disastrous extent in many parts of the world, and especially in the tropics.

Now that archæological enquiry has turned to the infrastructure of Maya life, investigating areas away from the ceremonial centres, the *milpa* view of ancient Maya agriculture has altered. It has been clear for several years that their methods were far more intensive and careful of natural resources than was originally supposed. Extensive networks of field walls and terraces (some from the Preclassic) show that much of the land was in long-term cultivation, with irrigation, drainage and erosion control all organized on a permanent basis. Recent discoveries of raised field systems (like the *chinampas* of Xochimilco and Chalco, which still provide most of the vegetables for Mexico City) show that this most intensive of farming arrangements was successfully used by the Maya. It involved raising artificial islands by dredging the water-courses round them, the dried weeds and mud adding each year to the fertility of the soil, as well as to its height above the water. It also seems likely that the canals thus created, and others specially dug, were stocked with fish, crustaceæ and edible molluscs, so that they were reservoirs of both food and drink.

The peoples of Mesoamerica have a long tradition of improving useful plants by means of selective breeding. It is known that the Maya succeeded in doubling the size of maize kernels in the Preclassic; other plants were similarly developed from exiguous wild beginnings. This talent can be observed among present-day people in highland Mexico, where a recent investigation found twelve different types of wheat being grown intentionally in one field, and 250 distinct varieties of cultivated bean in the same region. This apparently exaggerated profusion of plant strains should not be derided, for in it lies the best and safest promise for breeding types which will resist fungal and virus diseases. In some quarters this is regarded as new (or absurdly old-fashioned) wisdom, but who is to say that the Pre-Columbian farmers did not have some understanding of the matter?

Various fowls, notably turkeys, were domesticated by the ancient Maya, and there are records from colonial times that they kept tame deer, pigs and *techichi*, dogs bred for meat, although hunting was probably the main source of the darker meats. There was no stock raising or herding in the commonly accepted sense.

Representations of a bee-god, a rather mysterious multiple entity, give a hint of bee-keeping skills, as does a tradition of successful apiculture among the Maya of today.

The Maya were, and their rural descendants still are, keenly interested in wild plants. An American botanist in the 1930s, for example, found that his local guide could recognize 288 plant species and describe their specific uses.

One particular tree, the *ramon* or bread-nut *(Brosimum alicastrum)* was especially important as a food. Although rather dreary to eat, the seed of this tree lasts well in storage, for which the Maya constructed a special type of underground chamber called *chultún*. It must have given a much-needed elasticity to their economy, especially when the civic splendours of the Classic took so many labourers away from food production.

When the ceremonial centres in the rain forests were abandoned at the close of the Classic, it appears that the terraced fields were also abandoned. Similarly, in the drier north, the Postclassic brought in a more extensive mode of farming. A factor in this change may have been a conclusion on the part of the populace that it did not pay to produce much of a surplus as this led to the resulting spare time and extra production being commandeered for grandiose public works and uncomfortable warfare. These anti-feudal feelings have been expressed with some force in more recent times; indeed, they have been codified in the *ejido* system, by which almost the whole of post-revolutionary Mexico is divided into small-holdings.

El Tabasqueño has been cursorily explored, but never restored. The building illustrated appeared to be on the point of collapse in 1984. It stands in thick forest deep in rural Campeche.

EL TABASQUEÑO – *Principal Temple*

THE SITE OF ETZNÁ

To judge from the size and number of its buildings, Etzná was a most important centre in Classic times, with a suzerainty extending over hundreds of square miles. Long Count dates of that time are supplied by stelæ inscriptions, and there is sufficient archæological evidence to fix the building of the latest stage of the largest pyramid (here illustrated) in the seventh century AD. At the other end of Etzná's time span, finds of pottery beneath the open space in the foreground of the picture reveal an occupation at least as early as 1500 BC.

The monumental zone does not seem particularly extensive until one climbs the steps of this building, to look out over the thick forest which stretches away into the level distances of Campeche. Then one sees that the treetops rise near and far in several great surges, each one marking the presence of a large temple mound in the woodland beneath. Most of them have not yet been investigated; and if one goes to look for them at ground level, it is hard to recognize the work of man anywhere, so tumbled and overgrown are the ruins by their centuries of reclusion. Masses of smaller remains, now more or less level with the earth, lie between the more important structures. There was at least one ball court at Etzná, and a system of navigable canals which are also supposed to have served an intensive agriculture and probably to have contained fish, edible snails and other aquatic creatures for food.

The later buildings of this and other sites in the region are of an architectural type called Chenes, characterized mainly by the use of pillars, employed structurally in portals and ornamentally on façades. In its earlier periods, Etzná appears to have been strongly influenced by the Maya centres in the Petén: for instance, there is a pyramid inside the one illustrated, the oldest of three or possibly four successive stages, which has re-entrant angles at the corners as well as other stylistic traits found repeatedly at Tikal and Uaxactún.

The last and grandest stage of this monument is unusual in having five terraces, the lower four with rows of rooms on both sides of the main stairway, the uppermost carrying a large sanctuary divided into five chambers, and crowned by a high roof-comb. At the time of its original splendour, the whole of the exterior stonework was covered with white and coloured stucco, of which traces remain in the less weathered parts. The pyramid rises sixty-six feet from the built-up acropolis on which it stands; the surmounting temple and

Aquatic tortoises

Etzná
Pyramid of Five Terraces

roof-comb add a further thirty-six feet. The roof-comb has stone tenons protruding from its vertical faces, embedded there to support large plaster figures and masks which have long since fallen away. The remains of a huge stone and stucco monkey were found among the rubble at the foot of the building.

There is a hieroglyphic inscription carved into the risers of the bottom four steps. Above them the main stairway divides round a portal, then goes up in four flights to the top terrace, the slopes of the flights alternating in steepness. The galleries on the second and third terraces are double, with a row of older rooms running behind the front ones and communicating with them through a wall which appears to have been part of an earlier façade, overlaid by the present one in the last rebuilding. In order to accommodate the full extent of the bottom terrace, an older temple at the side was cut away and partially buried, as the illustration shows.

Blue-headed Parrot *(Amazona farinosa)*

MUSIC

Musicians with their instruments silent are a disappointment, and thus it is with the Classic Maya. Regrettably little, at this late stage, can ever be known of the harmonies (or otherwise) that accompanied their celebrations. Painting, sculpture and the architecture itself provide copious insights into the appearance of Maya ritual, and even of the musicians themselves, but they have been silent for a millennium and one cannot be very hopeful in attempting to realize the sounds they uttered.

Ethnographic enquiry in this field leads up blind alleys. Practically all 'Indian' music in the Maya area turns out to be derived, far back, from European or Moorish originals, and even if some of it did stem from an aboriginal American source, one could hardly expect to recognize it as belonging to a great civilization after so many centuries of cultural lapse.

Is it possible to deduce the character of one art from another? If it is, perhaps one could assign some of the harmony and rightness of Maya art and architecture to their music. Painstaking and careful to avoid æsthetic solecism in visual matters, they must have taken trouble in other fields as well and in this instance should surely be credited with something more than mere cacophany.

While their rhythms and melodies will not live again, there are records of some of the instruments they used and a hint of how some of them sounded. Bishop Landa's work of sixteenth century ethnography described the means of music-making then surviving in the Yucatán, stating that they were of long standing. The bishop's book is supplemented by other chronicles and by a splendid series of wall-paintings at Bonampak, not far from Yaxchilán in Chiapas. These murals are from the Classic period: they show several lively scenes, including a procession of people arrayed in their grandest dress and accompanied by a number of playing musicians. The impression given by all this evidence is that Maya music was strongly rhythmic, and made up entirely of wind and percussion instruments.

There were enormous and sonorous drums, presumably of wood, called *tunkul* (the largest being credited with a range of six miles), various smaller drums, including terracotta ones, and a great many rattles, which look in the pictures as if they were made from gourds. Rattles are mentioned among other instruments in accounts of their warfare, and one wonders if they were imitating the aggressive sound of the eponymous snake.

Wild pig *(Tayassu peccari)*

A noted percussive instrument was made from the empty plastron and carapace of a large marine turtle: Bishop Landa tells us that 'on being struck with the palm of the hand, it emits a sound which is both doleful and sad'. At Bonampak we see the same instrument being struck with a forked stick – or perhaps it is an antler.

Whistles were made from the leg-bones of deer and other animals, and trumpets, like Triton's wreathèd horn, from sea-conch shells. The chronicles tell of flutes and 'slight and sweet-toned trumpets' hollowed from reeds. The Bonampak murals show people blowing straight wooden horns three or four feet in length, with flared ends, while beside them are other long pipes, looking temptingly like bassoons, but probably percussion instruments (although the Lacandon Indians of modern Chiapas do play a type of reed oboe). The only authentic notes to survive are those to be got from a type of ocarina, almost a toy whistle, made of baked clay and occasionally turning up in excavations.

The remains of an unusual instrument survive at Chichén Itzá, a petrophone (like a xylophone, but stone instead of wood), perhaps better called a stone carillon. There are shuttle-shaped pieces of limestone up to four feet in length, with a deep groove running round one end so that they could be suspended on a frame with ropes. The stones lie in a pile but the looser ones give out a clear bell-like note when struck. Like a bell, each stone could only be tuned upwards, but the whole enormous instrument must have been capable of a lovely sound. If they were to be re-hung, one might be able to establish what musical scale was used by the ancient Maya.

How sad that the same Bishop Landa who recorded these matters, ordered the famous anti-idolatry-and-witchcraft bonfire at Muna in 1562, on which were burnt quantities of illustrated hieroglyphic texts in a disastrous *auto-da-fé:* some of those ancient books may well have touched on the music of Maya liturgies, by illustration or even with some kind of notation. As it is, no reconstruction is possible. Even the most scholarly attempt to suggest their strident war-music or the plangent strains of a royal funeral could be nothing but a bad guess, so far apart is our twentieth century world from theirs.

Late Preclassic toad basin in volcanic stone from Kaminaljuyu

Xlabpak is a minor site almost contiguous with Labná. This one extant building has been restored as far as the recovery of its components would allow. The style is typically Puuc, with strong geometrical patterns in the frieze, between tiered masks of the rain-god.

Xlabpak
Principal Temple

INSTRUMENTS FOR BUILDING

To lay out such very complicated buildings, the Maya must have had not only a good working knowledge of geometry but also some instruments to put it into practice. Without, it is hard to see how they could have accomplished such feats of architecture as the arrangement of internal stairways turning on themselves within solid structures, or the trapezoidal plans which give Classic Maya structures such a strange perspective. The disposition of elements on the buildings was generally performed with an elegance amounting to genius, and must have been accomplished with the aid of rulers, dividers and templates at the planning stage, and various sturdier devices during building.

For a builder, the most basic instruments of all are those which establish verticals and horizontals. The Maya must have had plumb-lines because their verticals were certainly accurate when they wanted them to be, even though so many walls were built with an inward or outward inclination. Horizontals up to the close of the Classic are almost always completely true, including the floors of the enormous *plazas* at places like Copán and Tikal, this precision being achieved with earthenware vessels specially made as water-levels. It is curious that these high standards were abandoned at late sites like Tulum, where no line is straight and all the surfaces slope up and down like soggy pastry.

The Maya also learnt to orientate their buildings with precision, happily for the numerous band of modern scholars who preoccupy themselves with astronomical alignments. As has been said in connection with Tikal, the lack of right angles in plan must surely have been intentional rather than accidental, and one can infer that the builders were well used to measuring angles and marking out the complementary ones.

Whether they first arrived at the proportions of their best buildings by calculation or by instinct, the Maya were helped by an advanced knowledge of arithmetic. Being vigesimal, it was better for builders than the decimal system, since their first higher unit, twenty, is divisible into four whole numbers, whereas with ten, one is all too quickly driven to fractions.

All that is known about the road-surveyors of the ancient world, including the Maya, is that they did not regard their far-reaching alignments as particularly difficult to achieve. With large forces at their disposal, they could establish a vague line quite quickly and then refine it with flags or fires until it was perfectly straight.

That they knew of the wheel is shown by some little wheeled toys found on the island of Jaina, but they never used it in a practical way. Everything heavy was rolled, pushed or dragged, unless it could be floated along by water. Woven and twisted ropes are depicted in their records, but there is no account of how they moved or raised the huge weights of their monuments. One assumes that very large stones were manœuvred across country on rollers (those useful causeways do not seem to have been in existence when they might have been most needed) and raised by means of levers, or perhaps taken up temporary ramps of earth. Any sort of sledge or arrangement of runners, such as was used by the ancient Egyptians, would have been hard to manage over much of the Maya terrain.

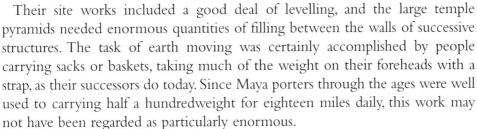

Ocelot *(Felis pardalis)*

Their site works included a good deal of levelling, and the large temple pyramids needed enormous quantities of filling between the walls of successive structures. The task of earth moving was certainly accomplished by people carrying sacks or baskets, taking much of the weight on their foreheads with a strap, as their successors do today. Since Maya porters through the ages were well used to carrying half a hundredweight for eighteen miles daily, this work may not have been regarded as particularly enormous.

The labours of stonework were divided into cutting down and roughing out large stones at the quarry, and performing the detailed carving at the building site. Quarry drilling does not seem to have been practised, but they did use the sequel to that operation, splitting the slabs off the matrix with wedges. Whether they were shaping the beautiful green trachyte of Copán, or the softer limestones of the Yucatán, they had only one basic material with which to do it – the hardest available stone, flint or chert, with the rarer and more expensive obsidian for finer details. All these stones were fashioned into tools by pressure-flaking. Both flint (fashioned into tools at factory sites) and obsidian (volcanic glass) were traded all over the Maya area and beyond, the flint from what is now Belize and the obsidian from its sources in the highlands of present Guatemala. No metal was used for tools by the Classic Maya, and the only metal to enter their Postclassic world to any degree was gold, with a purely decorative application.

Labná is a site with several fine buildings, although much decayed. The famous arch has been carefully restored to the limits of certainty, leaving doubtful parts unfinished. The style of the whole place is essentially Puuc, thus named after the local hills. A modern minor road runs through this locality, past a row of almost contiguous Maya centres including Labná, Sayil, Xlabpak and Sabbacché.

Jaguar *(Panthera onca)*

Labná
Arch from the north-west

120

THE SITE OF UXMAL

When Chichén Itzá was taken over by Toltecs in the tenth century AD, Uxmal was similarly colonized by the Xiú, another people from Central Mexico. However, whereas the Classic period architecture of Maya Chichén was heavily overlaid by Toltec work, this did not happen at Uxmal because the Xiu preserved the temples and palaces of their predecessors and respected the established style when making their own additions to the site. The result is that Uxmal survives as a major grouping of Classic buildings, with styles deriving from the rain forest sites to the south, (Río Bec, Tikal, etc.), from the Chenes area (Etzná, Xcalumkín etc.) and from the more local Puuc region. All these influences are manifest in the enormous Pyramid of the Magician.

In the usual manner of Maya pyramids, the antecedent stages of this one were re-faced, and in two cases completely buried, until the whole edifice culminated towards the end of the Classic period in the fifth and topmost temple. The first temple is nearly at ground level and in Puuc style. The second is much higher and now only accessible via a modern excavation stairway on the south-east side of the pyramid. Its roofcomb survives, buried by later masonry, and a little of it can be seen by visitors through a hole in the floor of the temple above (the fifth). The third temple was built back to back with the second, the former facing north-west and the latter south-east. The fourth temple was built in front of the third, which thus became an inner sanctuary.

Both third and fourth show strong influences from the southern rain forest sites, Temple IV in particular having a fanged mask for a doorway. Temple V is in a more local style, and its main façade is for some reason asymmetrical. Temples I and II were completely buried by subsequent stages, but Temples III and IV are re-incorporated as effective elements in the final structure. The main stairway (north-west) is flanked by stepped masks of rain gods, and near the top a throne has the same motif, which is carried further by more masks up the corners of the temple with the fanged mouth doorway. The pyramid itself has an unusual elliptical plan.

This one building cannot give a full idea of the riches of the site. The extent of Uxmal is enormous and there are many splendid buildings, some restored or at least uncovered, and some still shrouded in plants and rubble.

Several richly ornamented structures are grouped round the Monastery Quadrangle (so called), almost at the foot of the Pyramid of the Magician. Further away is the colossal Governor's Palace, grand and simple in its main lines but having a decorated frieze of dazzling complexity. Some of the best products of Frederick Catherwood's genius are his illustrations of this building.

No survey of Uxmal, however, brief, would be complete without mention of the austere House of the Tortoises.[1] This building is reminiscent of the best architecture of classical Greece, sharing with that great tradition a disciplined harmony of form.

1. See Introduction page 23.

122

Uxmal
Pyramid of the Magician from the West

THE COASTAL FORTRESS OF TULUM

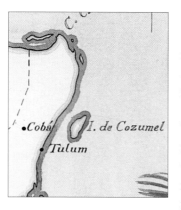

In the pale light of early morning Tulum on its cliff-top is a citadel of pearl. The waves below redouble the sunshine, giving the place its best aspect of the day, a wild seaward look and a maritime feeling rare among Maya monuments.

In fact the stout walls on the inland sides of Tulum show it to have been sited on the sea's edge for its better defence, rather than for easy access to the water. We know that coastwise trade was a feature of Maya life at the time of Tulum's main florescence in the Postclassic, but it is more a fortress than a port. Canoes could be pulled up on the small beach below the principal building, but unwelcome visitors would risk a vertical shower of stones.

The architecture of Tulum is disappointingly ramshackle and decadent. No wall runs level, no stone is cut quite to its best potential. Romantic though they look from afar, on a nearer approach the buildings are seen to be on a rather mean scale. The Classic Maya antecedents of the ornament at Tulum have been thoroughly coarsened by the unbeautiful influences of Toltec Chichén. There is little stylistic affinity with the large Classic site of Cobá, only a few miles inland, but then Cobá itself is an anomaly in that it derives more from the distant Petén zone of Guatemala than from such Yucatec contemporaries as Uxmal and early Chichén. In any case, Cobá in the Postclassic had declined considerably from its high Classic standards of architecture.

In one of the Tulum temples is seen an effigy of the 'diving god', even today recognized by the Yucatec Maya in the name of Xmulzencab, a god of bees and a patron of beekeepers. This divinity (in fact a plurality, like a community of hamadryads) has long been thought to dwell at Cobá, and the effigy occurs there and in other places along the east coast of the Yucatán.

Tulum has been identified with a thriving town mentioned by the earliest Spanish writers, but the evidence for such a late occupation is weak. The terns and frigate birds probably had the ruins to themselves for well over five hundred years, before Stephens and Catherwood discovered this old fort in the nineteenth century.

Maya house

TULUM
From the South

REFLECTIONS OF VIOLENCE

In his account of the Spanish conquest of Mexico, Francisco López de Gómara tells that at his request two soldiers counted the crania set out in neat rows on one of the enormous *tzompantli*, skull racks, in México-Tenochtitlán, and that they arrived at a figure of 136,000. The basement of this structure has been found and excavated. It accords with the early descriptions of it and there is no reason to suppose that the long vanished upper parts of wood were smaller than stated in the early chronicles. Perhaps the skulls were the accumulation of many years, but even so it is respectably estimated that the number of people sacrificed by the Aztecs exceeded 20,000 in the one year of 1520.

A smaller *tzompantli* survives at Chichén Itzá (the farthest building at the right hand side of the illustration). It was built in the twelfth century or thereabouts, after the Maya religion had been thoroughly altered by Toltec invaders. The vertical walls of the stone platform are adorned, if that is the word, with skulls in low relief, and testify, as do many other monuments of Toltec Chichén, to copious human sacrifice. The building next to the *tzompantli* has a frieze of eagles and jaguars devouring human hearts, and the ball-court has long sculpted panels, beautifully composed but of baleful content – scenes of solemn ceremony with ritual sacrifice at its centre.

The more exalted personages to be offered to the gods in this way were volunteers, who considered such a death the greatest honour attainable on earth. Their willingness may not have been shared by more than a small minority, but it does indicate sincerity. Clearly, it was felt that only the most extravagant offerings could avert cosmic catastrophe, especially at the turning point of one of the great time cycles when bad omens seemed to be accumulating – as in Mexico in 1520. The fear these martial and brave people had for the natural world seems quite reasonable, certainly understandable, when one considers the violence of the elements in Mexico and Central America. Ordinary tempests are generally no more severe there than anywhere else in the tropics, but the earth's crust is outstandingly unstable, the whole region being perpetually pregnant with volcanic activity. The Yucatán is less volatile than the rest of the mainland, but all the peoples of America must have known about seismic calamity.

Some examples. In 1982, the notorious volcano of El Chichón devastated a huge area near San Cristóbal de las Casas and covered much of the state of Chiapas with volcanic ash. In 1943, a volcano rose from a small fissure in a maize field not far from Uruapán in Central Mexico, forming a cinder cone 550 feet high within a week and becoming the present 2000 foot mountain of Paracutín after a year of violent eruption. Most dramatic of all in the centuries

Sulphur-breasted Toucan
(Rhamphastos sulfuratus)

since Columbus was the appearance in 1759 of the volcano Jorullo, in the Mexican state of Michoacán. The country round about received its first warning in the shape of fifty days of earthquakes, then, after a lull of a month or so, a large dome rose in the earth's surface. Various cones formed on the outside of this great bubble and spouted boiling mud and burning gases. Streams in the area were blocked by the movement of the earth and presently a tremendous explosion resulted from the meeting of their water with the incandescent contents of the volcano. There followed a period of terrifying electrical storms, the earth was again convulsed, and six more great domes appeared, the largest reaching a height of 1500 feet. Continual eruptions in the following year brought Jorullo to its present height of 4260 feet.

With this sort of thing liable to happen at any moment, quite unconnected with the seasons of the year, one cannot wonder that the ancient people of these lands spent such energy and application on astrology and divination, not to mention the hecatombs slain by some groups in an attempt to save their race. It is understandable that they should have predicted several ages for the world, each with its own particular destruction. How easy it must have been to view any period of apparent calm with apprehension – the longer the calm the greater the apprehension, and the more copious the sacrifice required to stave off disaster.

Chichén Itzá and Chichén Viejo really make up one very large site, with various groups of important buildings standing around and between them. The extent of the settlement, which includes many unexcavated buildings, is about three square miles.

CHICHÉN ITZÁ
Ball Court,
Temple of the Jaguars,
Tzompantli and
Platform of Jaguars
and Eagles

THE SITE OF CHICHÉN ITZÁ

There is no surface water in this part of the Yucatán peninsula, as the earth is so permeable. The location of Chichén is due to the presence of two *cenotes,* sink-holes, where the limestone crust has been undermined by water-filled cavities beneath, leaving large natural wells, whose water level is over forty feet below the surface of the site. The water itself is a further forty feet in depth, with ten feet of mud below that. This supply enabled a large population to live in the vicinity, but, remarkably, there is no evidence in the form of broken water pots to show that the larger *cenote* was ever used for domestic water, being left for sacred uses.

The site was first populated in the Preclassic period, probably as early as 1000 BC. There are several fine buildings at Chichén from the Classic period, which began there about AD 450 and closed with the arrival of Toltec invaders at the close of the tenth century. Among the finest of these purely Maya structures is the small temple known as La Iglesia, illustrated here, which stands at the edge of a group of similar age and style. The ornament is heavy, with masks of the Maya rain god prominent on all four façades. It has been ascribed to the eighth century or thereabouts.

The Toltec invasion of Chichén was accomplished with considerable violence, celebrated in wall-paintings in the Temple of the Jaguars (beside the Ball-Court), and on various artefacts, including some gold repoussé discs dredged from the mud in the largest *cenote.* The Toltecs were clearly a harsher people than their predecessors. Their religious and political system demanded spectacular conquest and sacrifice and this is reflected in the style of their architecture, which has harder lines and, one could say, a more threatening aspect than that of the Maya. While some Classic buildings were left unaltered by the Toltecs, and presumably used by them, others, like the Castillo, or Temple of Kukulkán, and the Caracol,[1] were overlaid or remodelled by the newcomers. In any case, all these buildings were utterly dominated by the purely Toltec architecture of the Ball-Court complex[2] and the Temple of the Warriors, huge, imposing and with a disquietingly totalitarian air about it.

The remarkable Maya skills of masonry and sculpture passed into the new era, so that Toltec Chichén is a far more impressive place than Tula, which the Toltecs left behind them on their departure for the Yucatán.

As a political state Toltec Chichén was destroyed in about AD 1200, but its Postclassic occupation continued until 1441, close enough to the arrival of the Spaniards in the following century for Bishop Landa to encounter many traditions concerning the place, which he included in his famous book, '*Relación de las Cosas de Yucatán*'.

1. See Introduction page 35 for illustration
2. See previous page for illustration

CHICHÉN ITZÁ – 'La Iglesia'

THE TEMPLE OF THE LINTELS AT CHICHÉN VIEJO

Anciens régimes have a certain appeal, conjuring as they do shades of sympathetic nobility dispossessed by vandals. And so it is at Chichén Itzá, where the Maya were overrun by the Toltecs. Judging by their monuments, architecture and other remains, the Toltecs seem to have been a harsh people, carrying militarism to cruel extremes. If we have an antipathy towards them on these grounds, it is reinforced at Chichén by a comparison between the purely Maya architecture and the more recent Toltec-Maya structures. The former seems far more humane than the latter; and the pains of subjugation endured by the Maya in the eleventh century are never long out of mind as one tours the site.

These feelings tend to enhance any appreciation of the Temple of the Lintels, an entirely Maya structure from the Classic period, in the group of buildings known as Chichén Viejo, some way south of the main part of Chichén Itzá. As the visitor is obliged to walk there, it is not greatly frequented, and offers a welcome solitude after the uproar of tourism near the main road. One goes and returns along a derelict Decauville railway line, haunted by flocks of bluebirds and huge iridescent butterflies.

The temple itself has been carefully restored by the Carnegie Institution of Washington, to the nearly complete condition in which it is now seen. Fortunately, nearly all the elements which had fallen from the building in its decay were found near at hand and could thus be replaced.

In this fine piece of architecture, richness is combined with restraint, and disciplined intervals with a sumptuous use of relief. The success of the building rests mainly on the harmony of its proportions, with an interplay of shadowed and sunlit surfaces producing a descant on the same theme.

Maguey *(Agave americana)*

CHICHÉN VIEJO
Temple of the Lintels

The basal platform has a strong but simple lattice pattern running between huge masks at the ends, these masks having a static character, like lurking toads, in contrast to the rain-god masks above, which exhibit a dynamism appropriate to their commanding position. The main wall at doorway level is unadorned, save by discreet engaged columns at the four corners. Above it runs a typically Maya architrave, with a zig-zag pattern inclined upward into the sunlight, representing a serpent of vast length. Then there is the frieze, which is the principal band of ornament. The rain-god masks face outwards, and between them run six panels of stone latticing separated by groups of engaged columns. The composition is capped by a simple and strongly modelled cornice. The three doorways, whose lintels inscribed with hieroglyphs gave the building its name, lead to three separate rooms within. Traces of coloured plaster, chiefly red and yellow ochre, remain in interstices of the exterior stonework. Long ago, when this colour scheme was complete, the effect must have been stunning – today's visitor must be content with the warm honey colour of the weathered stone.

One can only guess at the symbolism of the latticing and the columns. Both may be stylized recollections of domestic structures, but it will be noticed that the columns on the front of the frieze add up to twenty, a number of special significance to the Maya. The groups of columns used so often by the Maya on their façades may share a tradition with the stone sculptures called *atados de años* found buried in Aztec temples. These represented canes in bundles of fifty-two, the number of years in the most important Aztec time-cycle.

Mexican White Hawk (*Leucopternis alba*)

COBÁ AND ITS FIVE LAKES

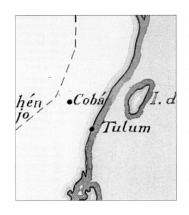

Cobá is twenty-seven miles from the sea in northern Quintana Roó. It is a huge place made up of several separate groups of important buildings, with dependent settlements extending in all directions, each with its principal house made of stone. Most of the site has never been excavated, and lies buried in thick forest, except where modern farming has made small clearances. The ancient Maya were attracted here by five contiguous lakes, unusual in a region whose subsoil is mostly porous limestone. The name Cobá Kinchil means 'waters ruffled by the wind'.

Culturally and economically the site was at its most powerful in the late Classic period, although occupation continued (possibly after an interruption) right through the Postclassic.[1] The Classic buildings have all been overlaid by later structures. This is sad from an æsthetic point of view, as the later architecture is for the most part rough and undistinguished, as at Tulum and similar sites on the nearby coast. However, two pyramids, impressive for their size alone, rise above tree level, at some distance from each other; others, as yet uncleared, are seen merely as wooded hillocks.

There are numerous stelæ both carved and plain, the latter when new having been plastered and then decorated with paintings. The custom at Cobá in the Classic era was to raise these monuments in the shelter of buildings, but every one of the standing stones was later removed from its original Classic position and re-erected in a new place during the Postclassic, showing that these dynastic memorials were valued and probably revered hundreds of years after the events recorded on them. Cobá seems to have been a forerunner of the northward movement in the tenth century AD of what may be termed the epicentre of Maya culture. The designs of the stelæ and of the Classic substructures of the buildings are similar in style to those seen at the Petén sites in Guatemala.

An unusual feature of Cobá is its network of roads. Two of these, perhaps the first two to be made, cross at right angles, suggesting an astronomical significance. The longest runs westward for sixty-three miles to Yaxuná, a minor site not far from Chichén Itzá. The terminus of the second longest is at Ixil, thirteen miles to the south-west. Another eight roads vary in length between just over a mile and four miles. All have outward termini of some sort, and their inner ends arrive on *plazas* with major buildings. The road widths also differ, but all give evidence of similar careful construction. Where the land dips, they are built up as causeways, sometimes fifteen or twenty feet above ground level, and they are provided with access ramps and branch

Cobá
Structure 1 from
Lake Cobá

Ruin at Sayil

avenues. The Yaxuná road has underpass tunnels, corbel-vaulted in the Maya manner, connecting farm land on either side. The main purpose of the roads has been the subject of much conjecture although the general view now is that they served to emphasize the spiritual and temporal ascendancy of the governing class in the ceremonial centre, focusing the surrounding population and their produce and conversely enabling authority to be exercised easily from its source. Moreover, the masses of labourers commuting to state building works would have been got to their tasks more speedily than in the days of rough paths through the bush.

One wonders why there was no proper road to the coast, since the sea was so near and goods were traded busily from that direction. The only reasonable answer seems to be that the Cobá people did not want access from that side to be too easy, in case they should be visited by invaders from abroad. Considering what eventually did take place with the arrival of the Spaniards, how wise they were. As it turned out, while all the early Spanish expeditions from Cuba, including that of Cortés, put in at nearby Cozumel and sailed along the coast, Cobá remained undetected in the hinterland until the Yucatán was overwhelmed by land-based forces later on.

---

1. At Cobá the Classic is considered to continue unusually late, AD 1100. The Postclassic runs from AD 1100 to the Spanish conquest.

A LONG VIEW

As regards their political thought, the Maya have the edge on us in one respect in that they seem to have taken an extremely long view of things. They considered a remote past, albeit through thick mists of legend, and the very long-term future was also a matter for serious speculation. Their talent for mathematics and their energetic search for order in the universe led them to discover all manner of astronomical cycles, observed and tabulated to a sharp point of accuracy. Hieroglyphic texts were composed to link those great sidereal revolutions with cycles of human fortune, and immense almanacs came into being, marked off in periods of good and bad augury for millennia ahead. The message of these forewarnings appears to have been a generally hopeless one: some people wiser and luckier than the rest might manage to circumvent disaster, but disaster there would be, by fire and flood, tempest and earthquake. Although mankind could hardly dare to stand up against the divine power of the elements, at least advocates and protectors could be found in the Maya pantheon, to bring some of the devout through each cataclysm and into calmer times. Even so, the people were to remain aware that the storms and eruptions would recur in an everlasting cycle of cosmic violence interspersed with regrettably few periods of peace.

What a contrast to the modern world, whose temporal prophets deem it highly inexpedient to forecast even the next trade recession when matters seem for the moment to be improving. The Age of Enlightenment cleared away not only a great body of superstition, but also a valuable tradition of humility in the face of the unknown.

An aptitude for seeing things cyclically was linked in the Maya to a habit of discerning the potential of their fellow creatures rather than simply their actuality. It seems that the Maya's knowledge of his surroundings was characterized by a keen appreciation of values, of uses, of possible latent powers. For instance, a dull little plant might heal (and in the end they knew the curative or culinary properties of hundreds of them), every timber was suited to at least one purpose, a jaguar (to them) had terrifying powers of metamorphosis. Of course magical matters were apt to muddle the pursuit of truth, but habits of speculation and experiment led to a respect for the natural world which European-based culture sadly lacks. It is a matter of great reproach that the Maya guides working for the botanist Cyrus Lundell in the 1930s should have known the nutritive or medicinal properties of 288 plant species while at the same time no proper survey of the timbers of those same woodlands had been attempted either by the national governments or by the timber concessionaires. It was already clear then that the usual system of

COBÁ
Pyramid of Nohuch Mul

logging was quite unnecessarily destructive, but the same system continues in many areas today. One can tell from the persistence of certain species at the ancient sites that the old Maya conserved what was useful to them. The contemporary lumberman, faced with his concession of tropical woodland, is infinitely more concerned with one crop, not of his own planting, than with a continuum, and this myopic selfishness is the main reason why tropical forests are still being destroyed. Admittedly, the recuperative powers of these forests were over-estimated until fairly recently, when their surprisingly low soil fertility came to be assessed, but commercial greed and an appalling hubris continue to rule the tropical timber trade in spite of every warning. One feels that the Maya astrologers would recognize in all this the approach of one of their cycles of disaster, and they might be right. It will do little good to look to the other side of the cycle, a doubtful recovery for those unhappy lands. Better, surely, to try and avert the day of wrath.

The building in the illustration is 138 feet high and the tallest pyramid in the Yucatán. It dates from the seventh or eighth century AD. The people engaged in the first excavations told the archæologists of a very ancient legend about a family of jaguars having lived for many years in the temple at the top. Some time later this was substantiated by a large find of appropriate animal bones which did not correspond to any period of human occupation.

All the earth is a grave and nothing escapes it;

Nothing is so perfect that it does not descend to the tomb.

Rivers, rivulets, fountains and waters flow

But never return to their joyful beginnings.

Anxiously they hasten to the vast realms of the Rain God:

As they widen their banks, they also fashion

The sad urn of their burial.

Filled are the bowels of the earth with pestilential dust,

Once flesh and bone, once the soul-endowed bodies of men

Who sat upon thrones, decided cases, presided in council,

Commanded armies, conquered provinces, possessed treasures, destroyed temples

Exulted in their pride, majesty, fortune, praise and power.

Vanished are these glories, just as the fearful smoke vanishes

That erupts so violently from the infernal fires of the volcano.

Nothing recalls them but the written page.

Nezahualcóyotl, King of Texcoco, AD 1402–1472.
(Translated from the Spanish of Fray Josef de Grenados y Gálvez, 1778.)

The watercolours illustrating this book were drawn and painted with huge admiration for the subjects and their creators. I found that Maya buildings and sculptures, especially in the Classic period, have an artistic and emotive strength that transcends their ruin. We know their government was at times tyrannical, but we also have evidence that all the pre-Columbian cultures of Mesoamerica had much in their social arrangements that was fine and enviable: deep respect for justice, for the old and sick, for women as members of society, for artists of every sort, for the natural world. I hope my regard for the Maya shows in this book and that readers will want to find out more about them and perhaps seek out some of the remains of their remarkable achievement. To be sure, the passing centuries have dimmed our vision of them: they themselves were keenly aware of mortality and the obliterating effects of time, a thought matchlessly expressed by the words (now twice translated) of Nezahualcóyotl, the 15th century poet and king of Texcoco in the Valley of Mexico, written before Columbus ever touched America.

Nigel Hughes
June 2000

SELECTED BIBLIOGRAPHY

Anon., *Maya Archæology*. Foundation for Latin American Anthropological Research, Guatemala.

Clissold, Stephen, *Latin America: A Cultural Outline,* Hutchinson, London, 1965.

Coe, Michael D., *The Maya*. London, Thames & Hudson, various editions. An excellent general account.

Díaz del Castillo, Bernal. *Historia Verdadera de la Conquista de la Nueva España,* translated as *The Conquest of New Spain,* Penguin 1963. Contemporary account of the Spanish arrival and conquest of Mexico.

Gendrop, Paul, *Los Estilos Río Bec, Chenes y Puuc,* UNAM, Mexico.

Graham, Ian, *The Art of Maya Hieroglyphic Writing.* Harvard University Press.

Hammond, Norman, *Ancient Maya Civilization.* Excellent general account.

Landa, Fray Diego de, *Relación de las Cosas de Yucatan,* Kraus Reprint Corporation, New York, 1966. Also published in a translation by A.M. Tozzer (Peabody Museum). The remains of a 16th century account of Maya culture, by the then Bishop of Mérida.

Lundell, Cyrus L., *Plants of the Petén,* Carnegie Institute. Botanical work in the 1930s with observations on ancient Maya culture, agriculture etc.

Marquina, Ignacio, *Arquitectura Prehispanica.* INAH, Mexico, 1964. Enormous technical catalogue of monuments, over the entire area of prehispanic culture in Mexico and Central America, with many photographs of buildings at the time of their first discovery.

Martinez, José Luis, *Nezahualcóyotl, Vida y Obra,* Fonda de Cultura Económica, México 1972.

Miller, Mary E., *The Art of Mesoamerica,* Thames & Hudson.

Portilla, M. León, *Aztec Thought and Culture,* University of Oklahoma, 1963.

Ranney, Edward, *Stonework of the Maya,* University of New Mexico.

Stephens, John L., *Incidents of Travel in Central America, Chiapas and Yucatan,* illustrated by Frederick Catherwood, 2 volumes, reprinted by Dover. Celebrated account of an exploratory journey by an American diplomat and an English artist in the 1830s.

Thompson, J. Eric S., *Maya Hieroglyphic Writing. An Introduction.* Also *Maya History and Religion.* University of Oklahoma Press.

Excellent site guides are generally available at the sites themselves – the more visited ones, that is. Examples include:

Coe, William R., *Tikal, A Handbook of the Ancient Maya Ruins,* University of Pennsylvania.

Fasquelle, Ricardo Agurcia, *Copán Ayer y Hoy,* Instituto Hondureño de Antropología e Historia.

Instituto Nacional de Antropología e Historia, *Guias Oficiales.* INAH, Mexico.

Pendergast, David M., *Altun Há.* The Government of Belize.

INDEX

(Page numbers in **bold** refer to main illustrations)

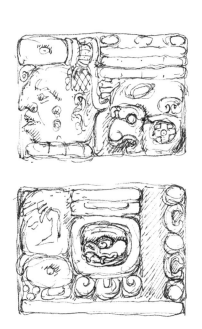